THE HISTORY OF THE NINETEENTH
CENTURY IN CARICATURE

E PLURIBUS UNUM

WHAT IT IS
AND
WHAT IS IT?

1861

THE HISTORY

OF THE

Nineteenth Century

In Caricature

BY

ARTHUR BARTLETT MAURICE

AND

FREDERIC TABER COOPER

PROFUSELY ILLUSTRATED

COOPER SQUARE PUBLISHERS, INC.
NEW YORK
1970

Originally Published 1904
Published by Cooper Square Publishers, Inc.
59 Fourth Avenue, New York, N. Y. 10003
Standard Book No. 8154-0342-9
Library of Congress Catalog Card No. 73-125160

Printed in the United States of America

To

HARRY THURSTON PECK

CONTENTS

CHAPTER   PAGE

PART I. THE NAPOLEONIC ERA

I. THE BEGINNING OF POLITICAL CARICATURE	1
II. HOGARTH AND HIS TIMES	12
III. JAMES GILLRAY	19
IV. BONAPARTE AS FIRST CONSUL	28
V. THE EMPEROR AT HIS APOGEE	35
VI. NAPOLEON'S WANING POWER	44

PART II. FROM WATERLOO THROUGH THE CRIMEAN WAR

VII. AFTER THE DOWNFALL	57
VIII. THE " POIRE "	65
IX. THE BAITING OF LOUIS-PHILLIPE	73
X. MAYEUX AND ROBERT MACAIRE	90
XI. FROM CRUIKSHANK TO LEECH	97
XII. THE BEGINNING OF PUNCH	101
XIII. RETROSPECTIVE	111
XIV. '48 AND THE COUP D'ETAT	119
XV. THE STRUGGLE IN THE CRIMEA	128

PART III. THE CIVIL AND FRANCO-PRUSSIAN WARS

XVI. THE MEXICAN WAR AND SLAVERY	143
XVII. NEGLECTED OPPORTUNITIES	159
XVIII. THE SOUTH SECEDES	166
XIX. THE FOUR YEARS' STRUGGLE	175
XX. NATIONS AND MEN IN CARICATURE	188
XXI. THE OUTBREAK OF THE FRANCO-PRUSSIAN WAR	197
XXII. THE DÉBÂCLE	206

vii

CONTENTS

CHAPTER   PAGE

PART IV. THE END OF THE CENTURY

XXIII. The Evolution of American Caricature . 231

XXIV. The Third French Republic . . . 236

XXV. General European Affairs 245

XXVI. Thomas Nast 255

XXVII. The American Political Campaigns of 1880
AND 1884 269

XXVIII. The Influence of Journalism . . . 278

XXIX. Years of Turbulence 289

XXX. American Parties and Platforms . . . 309

XXXI. The Spanish-American War 330

XXXII. The Boer War and the Dreyfus Case . . 342

XXXIII. The Men of To-day 355

LIST OF ILLUSTRATIONS

PAGE

What It Is and What Is It? . . . . *Frontispiece*

French Invasion of England 3

Nelson at the Battle of the Nile (Gillray) 5

Bonaparte after Landing (Gillray) 6

John Bull Taking a Luncheon (Gillray) 8

French Consular Triumvirate (Gillray) 11

Capture of the Danish Ships (Gillray) 14

The Broad-Bottom Administration (Gillray) . . . 16

Pacific Overtures (Gillray) 19

The Great Coronation Procession (Gillray) . . . 21

Napoleon and Pitt (Gillray) 23

Armed Heroes (Gillray) 25

The Handwriting on the Wall (Gillray) 27

The Double-Faced Napoleon (German cartoon) . . . 29

The Two Kings of Terror (Rowlandson) 31

The King of Brobdingnag and Gulliver (Gillray) . . 33

Napoleon's Burden (German cartoon) 36

The French Gingerbread Baker (Gillray) 38

The Devil and Napoleon (French cartoon) 39

The Consultation (French cartoon) 41

The Corsican Top in Full Flight 45

Napoleon in the Valley of the Shadow of Death (Gillray) . 47

The Spider's Web (Volk) 48

The Partition of the Map 49

Napoleon's Plight (French cartoon) 50

The Signature of Abdication (Cruikshank) 52

The Allies' Oven (French cartoon) 54

The New Robinson Crusoe (German cartoon) . . . 55

Napoleon Caged (French cartoon) 56

Restitution 58

Adjusting the Balance 60

John Bull's New Batch of Ships (Charles) 62

Russia as Mediator (Charles) 63

ix

PAGE

The Cossack Bite (Charles) 63
John Bull and the Alexandrians (Charles) 64
John Bull's Troubles (Charles) 64
The Order of the Extinguishers (French cartoon) . . 67
Proudhon 68
Digging the Grave 69
Le Poire (Philipon) 70
The Pious Monarch 74
The Great Nut-Cracker 75
Enfoncé Lafayette (Daumier) 77
The Ship of State in Peril 79
The Pit of Taxation (Grandville) 81
The Question of Divorce (Daumier) 83
The Resuscitation (Grandville) 84
Louis Philippe as Bluebeard (Grandville) 85
Barbarism and Cholera Invading 89
The Raid 89
Mayeux (Traviès) 91
Robert Macaire (Daumier) 93
Extinguished! 94
Louis Philippe as Cain 95
Laughing John—Crying John 96
The Wellington Boot 99
The Land of Liberty 103
England's Admonition (Leech) 104
The Napoleon of Peace 105
The Sea-Serpent of 1848 107
Europe in 1830 109
Honoré Daumier (Benjamin) 112
The Evolution of John Bull 115
Joseph Prudhomme (Daumier) 116
The Only Authorised Lamps (Vernier) 120
Italian Cartoon of '48 121
Napoleon le Petit (Vernier) 122
The New Siamese Twins 123
Louis Napoleon and Madame France 124
The Proclamation (Gill) 125
Split Crow in the Crimea 126
Bursting of the Russian Bubble 130

PAGE

General Février Turned Traitor (Leech) 131
Rochefort and His Lantern 133
Brothers in Arms 134
An American Cartoon on the Crimean War . . . 136
Theatrical Programme 138
The British Lion's Vengeance (Tenniel) 139
The French Porcupine (Leech) 141
Bank-Oh's Ghost, 1837 144
Balaam and Balaam's Ass 144
New Map of the United States 145
The Steeplechase for 1844 147
Uncle Sam's Taylorifics 150
The Mexican Commander 151
Defense of the California Bank 153
The Presidential Foot Race 153
Presidential Campaign of '56 154
No Higher Law 155
The Fugitive Slave Law 157
The Great Disunion Serpent 158
Rough and Ready Locomotive Against the Field . . . 160
Sauce for Goose and Gander 162
Peace (Nast) 164
Virginia Pausing 166
Civil War Envelopes 167
Long Abe 168
The Promissory Note 169
The Great Tight Rope Feat 170
At the Throttle 171
The Expert Bartender 172
The Southern Confederacy a Fact 173
The Brighter Prospect 174
" Why Don't you Take It? " 175
The Old Bull Dog on the Right Track 176
Little Mac in his Great Act 178
The Grave of the Union 180
The Abolition Catastrophe 181
The Blockade 182
Miscegenation 183
The Confederacy in Petticoats 184

PAGE

Uncle Sam's Menagerie 185
Protecting Free Ballot 186
The Nation at Lincoln's Bier (Tenniel) 187
Figures from a Triumph 189
The Diagnosis (Cham) 190
The Egerean Nymph (Daumier) 191
Paul and Virginia (Gill) 192
The First Conscript of France (Gill) 193
The Situation (Gill) 195
Louis Blanc (Gill) 197
Rival Arbiters (Tenniel) 198
The Man Who Laughs (Gill) 199
The Man Who Thinks (Gill) 200
" To Be or Not to Be " (Gill) 201
Achilles in Retreat (Gill) 202
The President of Rhodes (Daumier) 203
A Tempest in a Glass of Water (Gill) 204
A Duel to the Death (Tenniel) 205
September 4th, 1870 206
Her Baptism of Fire (Tenniel) 207
André Gill 208
The Marquis de Gallifet (Willette) 209
The History of a Reign (Daumier) 210
" This has Killed That " (Daumier) 211
The Mousetrap and its Victims (Daumier) . . . 211
Prussia Annexes Alsace (Cham) 213
Britannia's Sympathy (Cham) 214
Adieu (Cham) 215
Souvenirs and Regrets (Aranda) 216
The Napoleon Mountebanks (Hadol) 217
Prussia Introducing the New Assembly (Daumier) . . 219
" Let us Eat the Prussian " (Gill) 220
Design for a New Handbell (Daumier) 222
Germany's Farewell 223
Bismarck the First 224
Trochu—1870 225
Marshal Bazaine (Faustin) 226
Rochefort 227
The German Emperor Enters Paris (Régamey) . . . 228

PAGE

Caran D'Ache 232
Gulliver Crispi 233
Changing the Map (Gill) 234
Poor France! (Daumier) 237
The Warning (Daumier) 238
The New Year (Daumier) 239
The Root of all Evil 240
The Napoleonic Drama 241
The French Political Situation (Régamey) 243
New Crowns for Old 245
Tightening the Grip 246
Aeolus 247
" L'Etat, C'est Moi " 248
The Hidden Hand 249
The Irish Frankenstein 250
The Daring Duckling 251
Settling the Alabama Claims 252
Gordon Waiting at Khartoum 253
The Gratz Brown Tag to Greeley's Coat (Nast) . . . 256
Thomas Nast 257
Labour Cap and Dinner Pail (Nast) 259
The Rag Baby (Nast) 260
The Inflation Donkey (Nast) 261
The Brains of Tammany (Nast) 262
A Popular Verdict 263
The Tattooed Columbia (Keppler) 264
Splitting the Party 265
The Headless Candidates 266
On the Down Grade 267
Forbidding the Banns (Keppler) 270
The Wake (Keppler) 272
A Common Sorrow 273
Why They Dislike Him 274
The First Tattooed Man (Gillam) 275
A German Idea of Irish Home Rule 279
The New National Sexton 280
Horatius Cleveland 281
Bernard Gillam 282
Joseph Keppler 283

PAGE

The John Bull Octopus 285
The Hand of Anarchy 286
The Triple Alliance 287
A Present-Day Lesson 290
Gordon in Khartoum 291
The Spurious Parnell Letters 291
Dropping the Pilot (Tenniel) 292
L'Enfant Terrible 293
William Bluebeard 294
Chinese Native Cartoon 295
Japan in Corea 296
Business at the Deathbed 297
The Start for the China Cup 297
End of the Chinese-Japanese War 298
The Chinese Exclusion Act 299
The Great Republican Circus (Opper) 300
To the Rescue 301
A Pilgrim's Progress 302
General Boulanger 303
The Hague Peace Conference 303
A Fixture 304
Group of Modern French Caricaturists 305
The Anglo-French War Barometer 307
Rip Van Winkle Awakes 310
They're Off 311
Where am I at? (Gillam) 312
The Political Columbus (Gillam) 314
Cleveland's Map of the United States (Gillam) . . . 315
Return of the Southern Flags (Gillam) 317
The Champion Masher (Gillam) 319
The Harrison Platform (Keppler) 320
The Chilian Affair 322
A Political Tam O'Shanter (Gillam) 324
Don Quixote Bryan and the Windmill (Victor Gillam) . 325
Outing of the Anarchists 326
To the Death 327
The Great Weyler Ape 328
We are the People 329
Be Careful! It's Loaded (Victor Gillam) . . . 331

PAGE

The Safety Valve 333
The Latest War Bulletin (Hamilton) 334
Spanish Cartoons of the Spanish-American War . . . 335
The Spanish Brute (Hamilton) 337
Spanish Cartoons of the Spanish-American War . . . 339
The Rhodes Colossus (Sambourne) 342
The Situation in South Africa (Gillam) 343
Bloody Cartography 344
Lady Macbeth 345
The Flying Dutchman 346
Oom Paul's Favorite Pastime 347
Up against the Breastworks 348
The Napoleon of South Africa 349
Fire! 350
The Last Phase of the Dreyfus Case 350
Toward Freedom 351
The French General's Staff 352
Between Scylla and Charybdis 353
Devil's Island 354
C. G. Bush 356
Willie and His Papa (Opper) 357
Homer Davenport 359
Davenport's Conception of the Trusts 361

HISTORY OF THE NINETEENTH CENTURY IN CARICATURE

PART I

THE NAPOLEONIC ERA

CHAPTER I

THE BEGINNING OF POLITICAL CARICATURE

WHILE the impulse to satirize public men in picture is probably as old as satiric verse, if not older, the political cartoon, as an effective agent in molding public opinion, is essentially a product of modern conditions and methods. As with the campaign song, its success depends upon its timeliness, upon the ability to seize upon a critical moment, a burning question of the hour, and anticipate the outcome while public excitement is still at a white heat. But unlike satiric verse, it is dependent upon ink and paper. It cannot be transmitted orally. The doggerel verses of the Roman legions passed from camp to camp with the mysterious swiftness of an epidemic, and found their way even into the sober history of Suetonius. The topical songs and parodies of the Middle Ages migrated from town to town with the strolling minstrels, as readily as did the cycles of heroic poetry. But with caricature the case was very different. It may be that the man of the Stone Age, whom Mr. Opper has lately utilized so cleverly in a series of caricatures, was the first to draw rude and distorted likenesses of some unpopular chieftain, just as the Roman soldier of 79 A. D. scratched on the wall of his barracks in Pompeii an unflattering portrait of some martinet centurion which the ashes of Vesuvius have preserved until to-day. It is certain that the Greeks and Romans appreciated the power of ridicule latent in satiric pictures; but until the era of the printing press, the caricaturist was as one crying in a wilderness. And it is only with the modern co-operation of printing and photography that caricature has come into its full inheritance. The best and most telling cartoons are those which do not merely reflect current public opinion, but guide it. In looking back over a century of caricature, we are apt to overlook this distinction. A cartoon which cleverly illustrates some important historical event, and throws light upon the contemporary attitude of the public, is equally interesting to-day, whether it anticipated the event or was published a month afterward. But in order to influence public opinion, caricature must contain a certain element of prophecy. It must suggest a danger or point an interrogation. As an example, we may compare two famous cartoons by the English artist Gillray, " A Connoisseur Examining a Cooper " and the " King of Brobdingnag and Gulliver." In the latter, George III., in the guise of a giant, is curiously examining through his magnifying glass a Lilliputian Napoleon. There is no element of prophecy about the cartoon. It simply reflects the contemptuous attitude of the time toward Napoleon, and underestimates the danger. The other cartoon, which appeared several years earlier, shows the King anxiously examining the features of Cooper's well-known miniature of Cromwell, the great overthrower of kings. Public sentiment at that time suggested the imminence of another revolution,

Promised Horrors of the French INVASION. — or — Forcible Reasons for negotiating a Regicide PEACE. Vide *The history of Edmund Burke.*

GILRAY'S CONCEPTION OF THE FRENCH INVASION OF ENGLAND.

and the cartoon suggests a momentous question: "Will the fate of Charles I. be repeated?" In the light of history, the Gulliver cartoon is to-day undoubtedly the more interesting, but at the time of its appearance it could not have produced anything approaching the sensation of that of "a Connoisseur."

The necessity of getting a caricature swiftly before the public has always been felt, and has given rise to some curious devices and makeshifts. In the example which we have noted as having come down from Roman times, a patriotic citizen of Pompeii could find no better medium for giving his cartoon of an important local event to the world than by scratching it upon the wall of his dwelling-house after the fashion of the modern advertisement. There was a time in the seventeenth century when packs of political playing-cards enjoyed an extended vogue. The fashion of printing cartoons upon ladies' fans and other articles of similarly intimate character was a transitory fad in England a century ago. Mr. Ackermann, a famous printer of his generation, and publisher of the greater part of Rowlandson's cartoons, adopted as an expedient for spreading political news a small balloon with an attached mechanism, which, when liberated, would drop news bulletins at intervals as it passed over field and village. In this country many people of the older generation will still remember the widespread popularity of the patriotic caricature-envelopes that were circulated during the Civil War. To-day we are so used to the daily newspaper cartoon that we do not stop to think how seriously handicapped the cartoonists of a century ago found themselves. The more important cartoons of Gillray and Rowlandson appeared either in monthly periodicals, such as the *Westminster Magazine* and the *Oxford Magazine,* or in separate sheets that sold at the prohibitive

Extirpation of the Plagues of Egypt;—Destruction of 'Revolutionary Crocodiles;—or—The British Hero cleansing yͤ͢ Mouth of y͢ Nile.

NELSON DESTROYING THE FRENCH FLEET AT THE BATTLE OF THE NILE.

After Gillray.

price of several shillings. In times of great public excitement, as during the later years of the Napoleonic wars, such
cartoons were bought up greedily, the City vying with the
aristocratic West End in their patriotic demand for them.
But such times were exceptional, and the older caricaturists
were obliged to let pass many interesting crises because the
situations would have become already stale before the day

BUONAPARTE, 48 Hours after Landing!

of publication of the monthly magazines came round. With
the advent of the illustrated weeklies the situation was improved, but it is only in recent times that the ideal condition
has been reached, when the cabled news of yesterday is
interpreted in the cartoon of to-day.

There is another and less specific reason why caricature
had to await the advent of printing and the wider dissem-
ination of knowledge which resulted. The successful political

cartoon presupposes a certain average degree of intelligence in a nation, an awakened civic conscience, a sense of responsibility for the nation's welfare. The cleverest cartoonist would waste his time appealing to a nation of feudal vassals; he could not expect to influence a people to whom the ballot box was closed. Caricature flourishes best in an atmosphere of democracy; there is an eternal incompatibility between its audacious irreverence and the doctrine of the divine right of kings.

And yet the best type of caricature should not require a high degree of intelligence. Many clever cartoonists overreach themselves by an excess of cleverness, appealing at best to a limited audience. Of this type are the cartoons whose point lies in parodying some famous painting or a masterpiece of literature, which, as a result, necessarily remains caviare to the general. There is a type of portrait caricature so cultured and subtle that it often produces likenesses truer to the man we know in real life than a photograph would be. A good example of this type is the familiar work of William Nicholson, whose portrait of the late Queen of England is said to have been recognized by her as one of the most characteristic pictures she had ever had taken. What appeals to the public, however, is a coarser type, a gross exaggeration of prominent features, a willful distortion, resulting in ridicule or glorification. Oftentimes the caricature degenerates into a mere symbol. We have outgrown the puerility of the pictorial pun which flourished in England at the close of the seventeenth century, when cartoonists of Gillray's rank were content to represent Lord Bute as a pair of boots, Lord North as Boreas, the north wind, and the elder Fox with the head and tail of the animal suggested by his name. Yet personification of one kind and another, and notably the personifica-

tion of the nations in the shape of John Bull and Uncle Sam and the Russian Bear, forms the very alphabet of political caricature of the present day. Some of the most memorable series that have ever appeared were founded upon a chance resemblance of the subject of them to some natural object. Notable instances are Daumier's famous series of Louis Philippe represented as a pear, and Nast's equally clever, but more local, caricatures of Tweed as a money-bag. It would be interesting, if the material were accessible, to trace the development of the different personifications of England, France, and Russia, and the rest, from their first appearance in caricature, but unfortunately their earlier development cannot be fully traced. The underlying idea of representing the different nations as individuals, and depicting the great international crises in a series of allegories or parables or animal stories—a sort of pictorial Æsop's fables—dates back to the very beginning of caricature. In one of the earliest cartoons that have been preserved, England, France, and a number of minor principalities which have since disappeared from the map of Europe, are represented as playing a game of cards with some disputed island possessions as the stakes. In this case the several nations are indicated merely by heraldic emblems. The conception of John Bull was not to be evolved until a couple of centuries later. This cartoon, like the others of that time, originated in France under Louis XII. The further development of the art was decisively checked under the despotic reign of Louis XIV., and the few caricaturists of that time who had the courage to use their pencil against the king were driven to the expedient of publishing their works in Holland.

An impressive illustration of the advantage which the

satirical poet has over the cartoonist lies in the fact that some of the cleverest political satire ever written, as well as the best examples of the application of the animal fable to politics, were produced in France at this very time in the fables of La Fontaine.

The above are true Likenesses of CAMBACERES. LE BRUN. and ABBE SIEYES and BUONAPARTE, drawn at Paris Novr 1799

The French-Consular-Triumvirate, settling the New Constitution,
with a Peep at the Constitutional-Pigeon-Holes of the Abbe Sieyes in the Back Ground

BY GILLRAY.

CHAPTER II

FROM Holland caricature migrated to Great Britain in the closing years of the seventeenth century—a natural result of the attention which Dutch cartoonists had bestowed upon the revolution of 1688 —and there it found a fertile and congenial soil. The English had not had time to forget that they had once put the divine right of kings to the test of the executioner's block, and what little reverence still survived was not likely to afford protection for a race of imported monarchs. Moreover, as it happened, the development of English caricature was destined to be guided by the giant genius of two men, Hogarth and Gillray; and however far apart these two men were in their moral and artistic standards, they had one thing in common, a perennial scorn for the House of Hanover. Hogarth's contemptuous satire of George II. was more than echoed in Gillray's merciless attacks upon George III. The well-known cartoons of "Farmer George," and "George the Button-Maker," were but two of the countless ways in which he avenged himself upon the dull-witted king who had once acknowledged that he could not see the point of Gillray's caricatures.

Although Hogarth antedates the period covered by the present articles by fully half a century, he is much too commanding a figure in the history of comic art to be summarily dismissed. The year 1720 marks the era of the so-called "bubble mania," the era of unprecedented inflation, of the

South Sea Company in London, and the equally notorious Mississippi schemes of John Law in France. Popular excitement found vent in a veritable deluge of cartoons, many of which originated in Amsterdam and were reprinted in London, often with the addition of explanatory satiric verses in English. In one, Fortune is represented riding in a car driven by Folly, and drawn by personifications of the different companies responsible for the disastrous epidemic of speculation: the Mississippi, limping along on a wooden leg; the South Sea, with its foot in splints, etc. In another, we have an imaginary map of the Southern seas, representing " the very famous island of Madhead, situated in Share Sea, and inhabited by all kinds of people, to which is given the general name of Shareholders." John Law came in for a major share of the caricaturist's attention. In one picture he is represented as assisting Atlas to bear up immense globes of wind; in another, he is a " wind-monopolist," declaring, " The wind is my treasure, cushion, and foundation. Master of the wind, I am master of life, and my wind monopoly becomes straightway the object of idolatry." The *windy* character of the share-business is the dominant note in the cartoons of the period. Bubbles, windmills, flying kites, play a prominent part in the detail with which the background of the typical Dutch caricature was always crowded. These cartoons, displayed conspicuously in London shop windows, were not only seen by Hogarth, but influenced him vitally. His earliest known essay in political caricature is an adaptation of one of these Dutch prints, representing the wheel of Fortune, bearing the luckless and infatuated speculators high aloft. His latest work still shows the influence of Holland in the endless wealth of minute detail, the painstaking elaboration of his backgrounds, in which the most patient

British Tars, towing the Danish Fleet into Harbour; – the Broadbottom-Leviathan trying to swamp Billy's old Boat, & the little Corsican tottering on the Clouds of Ambition. –

"THE CAPTURE OF THE DANISH SHIPS."

By Gillray.

examination is ever finding something new. With Hogarth, the overcharged method of the Dutch school became a medium for irrepressible genius. At the hands of his followers and imitators, it became a source of obscurity and confusion.

While Hogarth is rightly recognized as the father of English caricature, it must be remembered that his best work was done on the social rather than on the political side. Even his most famous political series, that of " The Elections," is broadly generalized. It is not in any sense campaign literature, but an exposition of contemporary manners. And this was always Hogarth's aim. He was by instinct a realist, endowed with a keen sense of humor—a quality in which many a modern realist is deficient. He satirized life as he saw it, the good and the bad together, with a frankness which at times was somewhat brutal, like the frankness of Fielding and of Smollett—the frankness of the age they lived in. It was essentially an outspoken age, robust and rather gross; a red-blooded age, nurtured on English beef and beer; a jovial age that shook its sides over many a broad jest, and saw no shame in open allusion to the obvious and elemental facts of physical life. Judged by the standards of his day, there is little offense in Hogarth's work; even when measured by our own, he is not deliberately licentious. On the contrary, he set an example of moderation which his successors would have done well to imitate. He realized, as the later caricaturists of his century did not, that the great strength of pictorial satire lies in ridicule rather than in invective; that the subtlest irony often lies in a close adherence to truth, where riotous and unrestrained exaggeration defeats its own end. Just as in the case of " Joseph Andrews," Fielding's creative instinct got the upper hand of the parodist, so in much of

"BONAPARTE AND HIS ENGLISH FRIENDS—THE BROAD BOTTOM ADMINISTRATION."

By Gillray.

Hogarth's work one feels that the caricaturist is forced to yield place to the realistic artist, the student of human life, carried away by the interest of the story he has to tell. His chief gift to caricature is his unprecedented development of the narrative quality in pictorial art. He pointed a road along which his imitators could follow him only at a distance.

With the second half of the eighteenth century there began an era of great license in the political press, an era of bitter vituperation and vile personal abuse. Hogarth was one of the chief sufferers. After holding aloof from partisan politics for nearly half a century, he published, in 1762, his well-known cartoon attacking the ex-minister, Pitt. All Europe is represented in flames, which are spreading to Great Britain in spite of the efforts of Lord Bute, aided by his Highlanders, to extinguish them. Pitt is blowing upon the flames, which are being fed by the Duke of Newcastle from a barrow full of *Monitors* and *North Britons,* two scurrilous papers of the day. The bitterness with which Hogarth was attacked in retaliation and the persistence of his persecutors resulted, as was generally believed at the time, in a broken heart and his death in 1764.

An amazing increase in the number of caricatures followed the entry of Lord Bute's ministry into power. They were distinguished chiefly by their poor execution and gross indecency. As early as 1762, the *Gentleman's Magazine,* itself none too immaculate, complains that " Many of the representations that have lately appeared in the shops are not only reproachful to the government, but offensive to common-sense; they discover a tendency to inflame, without a spark of fire to light their own combustion." The state of society in England was at this time notoriously immoral and licentious. It was a period of hard living and hard drinking.

The well-known habits of such public figures as Sheridan and Fox are eminent examples. The spirit of gambling had become a mania, and women had caught the contagion as well as men. Nowhere was the profligacy of the times more clearly shown than in the looseness of public social functions, such as the notorious masquerade balls, which a contemporary journal, the *Westminster Magazine,* seriously decried as " subversive of virtue and every noble and domestic point of honor." The low standards of morals and want of delicacy are revealed in the extravagance of women's dress, the looseness of their speech. It was an age when women of rank, such as Lady Buckingham and Lady Archer, were publicly threatened by an eminent judge with exposure on the pillory for having systematically enticed young men and robbed them at their faro tables, and afterward found themselves exposed in the pillory of popular opinion in scurrilous cartoons from shop windows all over London.

Pacific Overtures — or — a Flight from St CLOUD's — over the Water to Charley — a new Dramatic Peace now Rehearsing

CHAPTER III

AT a time when cheap abuse took the place of technical skill, and vulgarity passed for wit, a man of unlimited audacity, who was also a consummate master of his pencil, easily took precedence. Such a man was James Gillray, unquestionably the leading cartoonist of the reign of George III. Yet of the many who are to-day familiar with the name of Gillray and the important part he played in influencing public opinion during the struggle with Napoleon, very few have an understanding of the dominant qualities of his work. A large part of it, and probably the most representative part, is characterized by a foulness and an obscenity which the present generation cannot countenance. There is a whole series of cartoons bearing his name which it would not only be absolutely out of the question to reproduce, but the very nature of which can be indicated only in the most guarded manner. Imagine the works of Rabelais shamelessly illustrated by a master hand! Try to conceive of the nature of the pictures which Panurge chalked up on the walls of old Paris. It was not merely the fault of the times, as in the case of Hogarth. Public taste was sufficiently depraved already; but Gillray deliberately prostituted his genius to the level of a procurer, to debauch it further. From first to last his drawings impress one as emanating from a mind not only unclean, but unbalanced as well—a mind over which there hung, even at the beginning, the furtive shadow of that madness which at last overtook

The Grand Coronation Procession of NAPOLEONE the 1ˢᵗ Emperor of France, from the Church of Notre-Dame, Dec. 2ᵈ 1804.

jam nova progenies cœlo demittitur alto.

Sic itur ad Astra.

Procul ô procul este profani.

Jam mora dicunt SATANA regna.

Berthier. Bernadotte, Augereau. &c all the brave Train of Republican Generals, marching in ô Procession. —

Puissant Continental Powers Train-Bearers to the Emperor

Ladies of Honor. (widows & Professors) — Train-Bearers to ô Empress

His Imperial Majesty NAPOLEONE ô 1ˢᵗ — & the Empress Josephine

His Holiness Pope PIUS VII conducted by his old Faithful Friend, Cardinal Feseli, offering ô Incense

Talleyrand Perigord. Prime Minister & King at Arms bearing the Emperors Genealogy.

"THE GREAT CORONATION PROCESSION OF NAPOLEON."

By Gillray.

and blighted him. There is but one of the hallmarks of great caricature in the work of Gillray, and that is the lasting impression which they make. They refuse to be forgotten; they remain imprinted on the brain, like the obsession of a nightmare. While in one sense they stand as a pitiless indictment of the generation that tolerated them, they are not a reflection of the life that Gillray saw, except in the sense that their physical deformity symbolizes the moral foulness of the age. Grace and charm and physical beauty, which Hogarth could use effectively, are unknown quantities to Gillray. There is an element of monstrosity about all his figures, distorted and repellent. Foul, bloated faces; twisted, swollen limbs; unshapely figures whose protuberant flesh suggests a tumefied and fungoid growth—such is the brood begotten by Gillray's pencil, like the malignant spawn of some forgotten circle of the lower inferno.

It would be idle to dispute the far-reaching power of Gillray's genius, perverted though it was. Throughout the Napoleonic wars, caricature and the name of Gillray are convertible terms; for, even after he was forced to lay down his pencil, his brilliant contemporaries and successors, Rowlandson and Cruikshank, found themselves unable to throw off the fetters of his influence. No history of Napoleon is quite complete which fails to recognize Gillray as a potent factor in crystallizing public opinion in England. His long series of cartoons aimed at " little Boney " are the culminating work of his life. Their power lay, not in intellectual subtlety or brilliant scintillation of wit, but in the bitterness of their invective, the appeal they make to elemental passions. They spoke a language which the roughest of London mobs could understand—the language of the gutter. They were, many of them, masterpieces of pictorial Billingsgate.

The Plumb-pudding in danger :— or State Epicures taking un Petit Souper.

"— the great Globe itself and all which it inherit, is too small to satisfy such insatiable appetites."
— Vide MW. Le Tremendous .... 2 octavo ... etc.

"NAPOLEON AND PITT DIVIDING THE WORLD BETWEEN THEM."
By Gillray.

There is rancor, there is venom, there is the inevitable inheritance of the warfare of centuries, in these caricatures of Gillray, but above all there is fear—fear of Napoleon, of his genius, of his star. It has been very easy for Englishmen of later days to say that the French never could have crossed the Channel, that there was never any reason for disquiet; it was another matter in the days when troops were actually massing by thousands on the hills behind Boulogne. You can find this fear voiced everywhere in Gillray, in the discordance between the drawings and the text. John Bull is the ox, Bonaparte the contemptible frog; but it is usually the ox who is bellowing out defiance, daring the other to " come on," flinging down insult at the diminutive foe. " Let 'em come, damme! " shouts the bold Briton in the pictures of the time. " Damme! where are the French bugaboos? Single-handed I'll beat forty of 'em, damme! " Every means was used to rouse the spirit of the English nation, and to stimulate hatred of the French and their leader. In one picture, Boney and his family are in rags, and are gnawing raw bones in a rude Corsican hut; in another we find him with a hookah and turban, having adopted the Mahometan religion; in a third we see him murdering the sick at Joppa. In the caricatures of Gillray, Napoleon is always a monster, a fiend in human shape, craven and murderous; but when dealing with the question of this fiend's power for evil, Gillray made no attempt at consistency. This ogre, who through one series of pictures was represented as kicked about from boot to boot, kicked by the Spaniards, the Turks, the Austrians, the Prussians, the Russians, in another is depicted as being very dangerous indeed. A curious example of this inconsistency will be found in placing side by side the two cartoons considered by many to be Gillray's best: " The King of Brobding-

"ARMED HEROES."

By Gillray.

nag and Gulliver," already referred to, and " Tiddy-Doll, the great French gingerbread Maker, Drawing out a new Batch of Kings." The " pernicious, little, odious reptile " whom George the Third is holding so contemptuously in the hollow of his hand, in the first caricature, is in the second concededly of European importance.

MENE MENE,
TEKEL,
UPHARSIN

J Gillray del

F W Fairholt F S A sc

"THE HANDWRITING ON THE WALL."

CHAPTER IV

BONAPARTE AS FIRST CONSUL

FOR the first decade of the nineteenth century there was but one important source of caricature, and one all-important subject — England and Bonaparte. America at this time counted for little in international politics. The revolutionary period closed definitely with the death of Washington, the one figure in our national politics who stood for something definite in the eyes of Europe. Our incipient naval war with France, which for a moment threatened to assign us a part in the general struggle of the Powers, was amicably concluded before the close of the eighteenth century. Throughout the Jeffersonian period, national and local satire and burlesque flourished, atoning in quantity for what it lacked in wit and artistic skill. Mr. Parton, in his "Caricature and Other Comic Art," finds but one cartoon which he thinks it worth while to cite—Jefferson kneeling before a pillar labeled "Altar of Gallic Despotism," upon which are Paine's "Age of Reason," and the works of Rousseau, Voltaire, and Helvetius, with the demon of the French Revolution crouching behind it, and the American Eagle soaring to the sky bearing away the Constitution and the independence of the United States, and he adds: "Pictures of that nature, of great size, crowded with objects, emblems, and sentences—an elaborate blending of burlesque, allegory, and enigma—were so much valued by that generation that some of them were engraved upon copper."

France, on the contrary, the central stage of the great

drama of nations, might at this time have produced a school
of caricaturists worthy of their opportunity—a school that
would have offset with its Gallic wit the heavier school of
British invective, and might have furnished Napoleon with
a strong weapon against his most persistent enemies, had he
not, with questionable wisdom, sternly repressed pictorial
satire of a political nature. As the century opens, the drama

" THE DOUBLE-FACED NAPOLEON."

From the collection of John Leonard Dudley, Jr.

of the ensuing fourteen years becomes clearly defined; the
prologue has been played; Napoleon's ambition in the East
has been checked, first by the Battle of the Nile, and then
definitely at Aboukir. Henceforth he is to limit his schemes
of conquest to Europe, and John Bull is the only national
figure who seems likely to attempt to check him. The Battle
of the Nile was commemorated by Gillray, who depicted

Nelson's victory in a cartoon entitled "Extirpation of the Plagues of Egypt, Destruction of the Revolutionary Crocodiles, or the British Hero Cleansing the Mouth of the Nile." Here Nelson is shown dispersing the French fleet treated as crocodiles. He has destroyed numbers with his cudgel of British oak; he is beating down others; a whole bevy, with hooks through their noses, are attached by strings to the iron hook which replaced his lost forearm. In the distance a crocodile is bursting and casting fire and ruin on all sides. This is an allusion to the destruction of the *Orient,* the flagship of the Republican Admiral, the heroic Brueys, who declined to quit his post when literally cut to pieces.

Another cartoon by Gillray which belongs to this period is "The French Consular Triumvirate Settling the New Constitution." It introduces the figures of Napoleon and his fellow-consuls, Cambacérès and Lebrun, who replaced the very authors of the new instrument, Sièyes and Ducos, quietly deposed by Napoleon within the year. The second and third consuls are provided with blank sheets of paper, for mere form—they have only to bite their pens. The Corsican is compiling a constitution in accordance with his own views. A band of imps is beneath the table, forging new chains for France and for Europe.

In England, the Addington ministry, which in 1801 replaced that of William Pitt, and are represented in caricature as "Lilliputian substitutes" lost in the depths of Mr. Pitt's jack-boots, set out as a peace ministry and entered into the negotiations with Napoleon which, in the following March, resulted in the Peace of Amiens. Gillray anticipated this peace with several alarmist cartoons: "Preliminaries of Peace," representing John Bull being led by the nose across the channel over a rotten plank, while Britannia's shield and

several valuable possessions have been cast aside into the
water; and " Britannia's Death Warrant," in which Britannia
is seen being dragged away to the guillotine by the Corsican
marauder. The peace at first gave genuine satisfaction in
England, but toward the end of 1802 there were growing
signs of popular discontent, which Gillray voiced in " The
Nursery, with Britannia Reposing in Peace." Britannia is
here portrayed as an overgrown baby in her cradle and fed
upon French principles by Addington, Lord Hawkesbury, and
Fox. Still more famous was his next cartoon, " The First

" THE TWO KINGS OF TERROR."
After a cartoon by Rowlandson.

Kiss this Ten Years; or, the Meeting of Britannia and Citizen
François." Britannia, grown enormously stout, her shield
and spear idly reposing against the wall, is blushing deeply
at his warm embrace and ardent expressions of joy:
" Madame, permit me to pay my profound esteem to your
engaging person, and to seal on your divine lips my everlast-
ing attachment! ! !" She replies: " Monsieur, you are
truly a well-bred gentleman; and though you make me blush,

yet you kiss so delicately that I cannot refuse you, though I was sure you would deceive me again." In the background the portraits of King George and Bonaparte scowl fiercely at each other upon the wall. This is said to be one of the very few caricatures which Napoleon himself heartily enjoyed.

From now on, the cartoons take on a more caustic tone. Britannia is being robbed of her cherished possessions, even Malta being on the point of being wrested from her; while the bugaboo of an invading army looms large upon the horizon. In one picture Britannia, unexpectedly attacked by Napoleon's fleet, is awakening from a trance of fancied peace, and praying that her " angels and ministers of *dis*grace defend her! " In another, John Bull, having waded across the water, is taunting little Boney, whose head just shows above the wall of his fortress:

> If you mean to invade us, why make such a rout?
> I say, little Boney, why don't you come out?
> Yes, d—— you, why don't you come out?

In his cartoon called " Promised Horrors of the French Invasion; or, Forcible Reasons for Negotiating a Regicide Peace," Gillray painted the imaginary landing of the French in England. The ferocious legions are pouring from St. James's Palace, which is in flames, and they are marching past the clubs. The practice of patronizing democracy in the countries they had conquered has been carried out by handing over the Tories, the constitution, and the crown to the Foxite reformers and the Whig party. The chief hostility of the French troops is directed against the aristocratic clubs. An indiscriminate massacre of the members of White's is proceeding in the doorways, on the balconies, and wherever the republican levies have penetrated. The royal princes are stabbed and thrown into the street. A rivulet of blood is

" You may have seen Gillray's famous print of him—
in the old wig, in the stout, old, hideous Windsor uniform—as the King of Brobdingnag, peering at a little
Gulliver, whom he holds up in his hand, whilst in the
other he has an opera-glass, through which he sur-
veys the pygmy? Our fathers chose to set up George
as the type of a great king ; and the little Gulliver was
the great Napoleon."—*Thackeray's " Four Georges."*

running.   In the center of the picture is a tree of liberty.
To this tree Pitt is bound, while Fox is lashing him.

The increasing venom of the English cartoons, and their
frequent coarse personalities, caused no little uneasiness to
Bonaparte, until they culminated in a famous cartoon by
Gillray, " The Handwriting on the Wall," a broad satire on
Belshazzar's feast, which was published August 24, 1803.
The First Consul, his wife Josephine, and the members of the
court are seated at table, consuming the good things of Old
England.   The palace of St. James, transfixed upon Napoleon's fork; the tower of London, which one of the convives
is swallowing whole; the head of King George on a platter
inscribed: " Oh, de beef of Old England! "   A hand above
holds out the scales of Justice, in which the legitimate crown
of France weighs down the red cap with its attached chain—
despotism misnamed liberty.

CHAPTER V

FOR the next year parliamentary strife at home, fostered by Pitt's quarrel with the Addington ministry on the one hand and his opposition to Fox on the other, kept the cartoonists busy. They found time, however, to celebrate the coronation of Napoleon as Emperor in December, 1804. Gillray anticipated the event with a cartoon entitled " The Genius of France Nursing her Darling," in which the genius, depicted as a lady with blood-stained garments and a reeking spear, tosses an infant Napoleon, armed with a scepter, and vainly tries to check his cries with a rattle surmounted by a crown.

Rowlandson, Gillray's clever and more artistic contemporary, commemorated the event itself in a clever cartoon, " The Death of Madame République," published December 14, 1804. The moribund République lies stretched upon her death-bed, her nightcap adorned with the tricolored cockade. The Abbé Sièyes, in the rôle of doctor, is exhibiting the Emperor, portrayed as a newborn infant in long clothes. John Bull, spectacles on nose, is regarding the altered conditions with visible astonishment. " Pray, Mr. Abbé Sièyes, what was the cause of the poor lady's death? She seemed at one time in a tolerable thriving way." " She died in childbed, Mr. Bull, after giving birth to this little Emperor ! "

This was followed on the 1st of January by a large satirical print by Gillray, of " The Grand Coronation Procession," in which the feature that gave special offense was the group of three princesses, the Princess Borghese, the Princess Louise, and the Princess Joseph Bonaparte, arrayed in garments of indecent scantiness, and heading the procession as the " three imperial Graces." The English caricatures of this period relating to the new Emperor and Empress are as a rule not

FROM A GERMAN CARTOON OF THE PERIOD.

only libelous, but grossly coarse. At the same time, the political conditions of the times are cleverly hit off in " The Plum Pudding in Danger; or, State Epicures Taking un Petit Souper," published February 26, 1805, which depicts the rival pretensions of Napoleon and Pitt. They are seated at opposite sides of the table, the only dish between them being the Globe, served up on a shallow plate and resembling a plum pudding. Napoleon's sword has sliced off the continent—France, Holland, Spain, Italy, Prussia—and his fork is dug spitefully into Hanover, which was then an appanage of the British crown. Pitt's trident is stuck in the ocean, and his carver is modestly dividing the Globe down the middle.

During the summer of 1805 the third coalition against France was completed, its chief factors being Great Britain, Russia, and Austria. A contemporary print entitled " Tom Thumb at Bay " commemorates the new armament. Napoleon, dropping crown and scepter in his flight, is evading the Austrian eagle, the Russian bear, and the Westphalian pig, only to run at last pell-mell into the gaping jaws of the British lion. It is somewhat curious that the momentous events of the new war—the annihilation of the French fleet at Trafalgar, the equally decisive French victory at Austerlitz—were scarcely noticed in caricature, and a few exceptions have little merit. But in the following January, 1806, when Napoleon had entered upon an epoch of king-making, with his kings of Wurtemburg and Bavaria, Gillray produced one of his most famous prints. It was published the 23d of January (the day that Pitt breathed his last), and was entitled " Tiddy-Doll, the Great French Gingerbread Baker, Drawing out a new Batch of Kings, His Man, ' Hopping Talley,' Mixing up the Dough." The great gilt gingerbread baker is shown at work at his new French oven for imperial gingerbread. He is just drawing from the oven's mouth a fresh batch of kings. The fuel is shown in the form of cannon-balls. Holland, Switzerland, Austria, Italy, Venice and Spain are following the fate of the French Republic. On top of the chest of drawers, labeled respectively " kings and queens," " crowns and scepters," " suns and moons " is arranged a gay parcel of little dough viceroys intended for the next batch.   Among them are the figures of Fox, Sheridan, Derby, and others of the Whig party in England.

In the comprehensive and ill-assorted Coalition ministry which was formed soon after Pitt's death, the caricaturists found a congenial topic for their pencils.   They ridiculed it

TIDDY-DOLL the great French Gingerbread-Baker, drawing out a new Batch of Kings.—Izn Mam Happung Tulley, miaing up the Dongh

unmercifully under the title " All the Talents," and the " Board Bottomed " ministry.   A composite picture by Row-landson shows the ministry as a spectacled ape in the wig of a learned justice, with episcopal mitre and Catholic crozier. He wears a lawyer's coat and ragged breeches, with a shoe on one foot and a French jack-boot on the other.   He is dancing on a funeral pyre of papers, the results of the administration, its endless negotiations with France, its sinecures and patron-ages, which are blazing away.   The creature's foot is dis-charging a gun, which produces signal mischief in the rear and brings down two heavy folios, the Magna Charta and the Coronation Oath, upon its head.

This ministry's futile negotiations for peace with France are frequently burlesqued. Gillray published on April 5 "Pacific Overtures; or, a Flight from St. Cloud's ' over the water to Charley,' " in which the negotiations are described as " a new dramatic *peace,* now rehearsing." In this cartoon King George has left the state box—where the play-book of " I Know You All " still remains open—to approach nearer

"THE DEVIL AND NAPOLEON."
From an anonymous French caricature.

to little Boney, who, elevated on the clouds, is directing attention to his proposed treaty. " Terms of Peace: Acknowledge me as Emperor; dismantle your fleet, reduce your armies; abandon Malta and Gibraltar; renounce all continental connection; your colonies I will take at a valuation; engage to pay to the Great Nation for seven years annually one million pounds; and place in my hands as hostages the Princess Charlotte of Wales, with others of the late administration whom I shall name." King George replies: " Very amusing terms, indeed, and might do vastly well with some of the new-made little gingerbread kings; but we are not in the habit of giving up either ships or commerce or colonies merely because little Boney is in a pet to have them." This cartoon introduces among others Talleyrand, O'Conor, Fox, Lord Ellenborough, the Duke of Bedford, Lord Moira, Lord Lauderdale, Addington, Lord Henry Petty, Lord Derby, and Mrs. Fitzherbert.

Shortly afterward, on July 21, 1806, Rowlandson voices the current feeling of distrust of Fox in " Experiments at Dover; or, Master Charley's Magic Lantern." Fox is depicted at Dover, training the rays of his magic lantern on the cliffs of Calais. John Bull, watching him, is not satisfied. " Yes, yes, it be all very fine, if it be true; but I can't forget that d—d Omnium last week. . . I will tell thee what, Charley, since thee hast become a great man, I think in my heart thee beest always conjuring."

The cartoon entitled " Westminster Conscripts under the Training Act " appeared September 1, 1806. Napoleon, the drill sergeant, is elevated on a pile of cannon-balls; he is giving his authoritative order to " Ground arms." The invalided Fox has been wheeled to the ground in his armchair; the Prince of Wales' plume appears on the back of his seat. Other figures in the cartoon are Lord Lauderdale, Lord Grenville, Lord Howick, Lord Holland, Lord Robert Spencer, Lord Ellenborough, the Duke of Clarence, Lord Moira, Lord Chancellor Erskine, Colonel Hanger, and Talleyrand.

Gillray has left a cartoon commemorating the arrival of the Danish squadron, under the title of " British Tars Towing the Danish Fleet into Harbor; the Broad Bottom

(Le Cardinal Fesch.)

La Consultation.

NAPOLEON : "Dear cousin, how do you find my condition?"
CARDINAL FESCH : "Sire, it cannot last. Your Majesty has too bad a constitution."

From the collection of John Leonard Dudley, Jr.

Leviathan trying to swamp Billy's Old Boat; and the Little Corsican Tottering on the Clouds of Ambition." This cartoon was issued October 1, 1807. Lords Liverpool and Castlereagh are lustily rowing the *Billy Pitt;* Canning, seated in the stern, is towing the captured fleet into Sheerness, with the Union Jack flying over the forts. Copenhagen, smoking from the recent bombardment, may be distinguished in the distance. In Sheerness harbor the sign of·" Good Old George " is hung out at John Bull's Tavern; John Bull is seated at the door, a pot of porter in his hand, waving his hat and shouting: " Rule Britannia! Britannia Rules the Waves!" That the expedition did not escape censure is shown by the figure of a three-headed porpoise which is savagely assailing the successful crew. This monster bears the heads of Lord Howick, shouting " Detraction! " Lord St. Vincent filled with " Envy," and discharging a watery broadside; and Lord Grenville, who is raising his " Opposition Clamor " to confuse their course.

CHAPTER VI

NO period of the Napoleonic wars gave better opportunity for satire than Napoleon's disastrous occupation of Spain and his invasion of Portugal. The titles alone of the cartoons would fill a volume. The sanguine hopes of success cherished by the English government are expressed by Gillray in a print published April 10, 1808. " Delicious Dreams! Castles in the Air! Glorious Prospects! " It depicts the ministers sunken in a drunken sleep and visited by glorious visions of Britannia and her lion occupying a triumphal car formed from the hull of a British ship, drawn by an Irish bull and led by an English tar. She is dragging captive to the Tower little Boney and the Russian Bear, both loaded with chains.

The dangers which threatened Napoleon at this period were shown by Gillray in one of the most striking of all his cartoons, the "Valley of the Shadow of Death," which was issued September 24, 1808. The valley is the valley of Bunyan's allegory. The Emperor is proceeding timorously down a treacherous path, bounded on either side by the waters of Styx and hemmed in by a circle of flame. From every side horrors are springing up to assail him. The British lion, raging and furious, is springing at his throat. The Portuguese wolf has broken his chain. King Death, mounted on a mule of " True Royal Spanish Breed," has cleared at a bound the body of the ex-King Joseph, which has been thrown into the " Ditch of Styx." Death is poising his spear with fatal

"THE CORSICAN TOP IN FULL FLIGHT."

From a colored stamp of the period.

aim, warningly holding up at the same time his hour-glass with the sand exhausted; flames follow in his course. From the smoke rise the figures of Junot and Dupont, the beaten generals. The papal tiara is descending as a " Roman meteor," charged with lightnings to blast the Corsican. The " Turkish New Moon " is seen rising in blood. The " Spirit of Charles XII." rises from the flames to avenge the wrongs of Sweden. The " Imperial German Eagle " is emerging from a cloud; the Prussian bird appears as a scarecrow, making desperate efforts to fly and screaming revenge. From the " Lethean Ditch " the " American Rattlesnake " is thrusting forth a poisoned tongue. The " Dutch Frogs " are spitting out their spite; and the Rhenish Confederation is personified as a herd of starved " Rats," ready to feast on the Corsican. The great " Russian Bear," the only ally Napoleon has secured, is shaking his chain and growling—a formidable enemy in the rear.

Gillray's caricature entitled " John Bull Taking a Luncheon; or, British Cooks Cramming Old Grumble-Gizzard with Bonne Chère," shows the strange-appearing John of the caricature of that day sitting at a table, overwhelmed by the zealous attentions of his cooks, foremost among whom is the hero of the Nile, who is offering him a " Fricassée à la Nelson," a large dish of battered French ships of the line. John is swallowing a frigate at a mouthful. Through the window we see Fox and Sheridan, representative of the Broad Bottom administration, running away in dismay at John Bull's voracity.

As Gillray retires from the field several other clever artists stand ready to take his place, and chief among them Rowlandson. The latter had a distinct advantage over Gillray in his superior artistic training. He was educated in the French

THE VALLEY OF THE SHADOW OF DEATH.

NAPOLEON IN THE VALLEY OF THE SHADOW OF DEATH.

From James Gillray's caricature.

schools, where he gave especial attention to studies from the nude. In the opinion of such capable judges as Reynolds, West, and Lawrence, his gifts might have won him a high place among English artists, if he had not turned, through sheer perversity, to satire and burlesque. Rowlandson's Napoleonic cartoons began in July, 1808. These initial efforts are neither especially characteristic nor especially

FROM A GERMAN CARICATURE COMMEMORATING
GERMAN SUCCESS IN 1814.

clever, but they certainly were duly appreciated by the public. Joseph Grego, in his interesting and comprehensive work upon Rowlandson, says of them:

"It is certain that the caricaturist's travesties of the little Emperor, his burlesques of his great actions and grandiose declarations, his figurative displays of the mean origin of the

imperial family, with the cowardice and depravity of its members, won popular applause. . . And when disasters began
to cloud the career of Napoleon, as army after army melted
away, . . . the artist bent his skill to interpret the delight
of the public.   The City competed with the West End in

"THE PARTITION OF THE MAP."
From the collection of John Leonard Dudley, Jr.

buying every caricature, in loyal contest to prove their
national enmity for Bonaparte.   In too many cases, the incen-
tive was to gratify the hatred of the Corsican rather than any
remarkable merit that could be discovered in the caricatures.
Very few of these mock-heroic sallies imprint themselves upon

the recollection by sheer force of their own brilliancy, as was the case with Gillray, and frequently with John Tenniel. Rowlandson and Cruikshank are risible, but not inspired."

On July 8 Rowlandson began his series with "The Corsican Tiger at Bay." Napoleon is depicted as a savage tiger, rending four "Royal Greyhounds," quite at his mercy. But a fresh pack appears in the background and prepares for a fierce charge. The Russian bear and Austrian eagle are securely bound with heavy fetters, but the eagle is asking: "Now, Brother Bruin, is it time to break our fetters?"

"The Beast as Described in the Revelations" followed

"THE CHIEF OF THE GRAND ARMY IN A SAD
PLIGHT."
From a French cartoon of the period.

within two weeks. The beast, of Corsican origin, is represented with seven heads, and the names of Austria, Naples, Holland, Denmark, Prussia, and Russia are inscribed on their respective crowns. Napoleon's head, severed from the trunk, vomits forth flames. In the distance, cities are blazing, showing the destruction wrought by the beast. Spain is represented as the champion who alone dares to stand against the monster.

"The Political Butcher" bears date September 12 of

the same year. In this print the Spanish Don, in the garb of a butcher, is cutting up Bonaparte for the benefit of his neighbors. The body of the late Corsican lies before him and is being cut up with professional zeal. The Don holds up his enemy's heart and calls upon the other Powers to take their share. The double-headed eagle of Austria is swooping upon Napoleon's head: " I have long wished to strike my talons into that diabolical head-piece "; the British bulldog has been enjoying portions of the joints, and thinks that he would " like to have the picking of that head." The Russian bear is luxuriously licking Napoleon's boots, and remarks, " This licking is giving me a mortal inclination to pick a bone."

The final failure of the Spanish campaign is signalized, September 20, in a cartoon labeled " Napoleon the Little in a Rage with his Great French Eagle." The Emperor, with drawn sword and bristling with rage, threatens the French imperial eagle, larger than himself. The bird's head and one leg are tied up—the result of damage inflicted by the Spaniards. " Confusion and destruction! " thunders Napoleon, " what is this I see? Did I not command you not to return until you had spread your wing of victory over the whole of Spain? " " Aye, it's fine talking," rejoins the bird, " but if you had been there, you would not much have liked it. The Spanish cormorants pursued me in such a manner that they set me molting in a terrible way. I wonder that I have not lost my feathers. Besides, it got so hot I could not bear it any longer."

In August, 1809, Rowlandson published " The Rising Sun." Bonaparte is surrounded by the Continental powers, and is busy rocking to sleep in a cradle the Russian bear, securely muzzled with French promises. But the dawn of a

"THE SIGNATURE OF ABDICATION."

From a caricature in color by George Cruikshank.

new era is breaking: the sun of Spain and Portugal is rising
with threatening import. The Emperor is disturbed by the
new light: " This rising sun has set me upon thorns." The
Prussian eagle is trussed; Denmark is snuffed out. But
Austria has once more taken heart: " Tyrant, I defy thee and
thy cursed crew ! "

The victories of the Peninsular war, and later of the
disastrous Russian campaign, called forth an ever-increasing
number of cartoons, which showed little mercy or consideration to a fallen foe. A sample of the titles of this period show
the general tendency; he is the " Corsican Bloodhound," the
" Carcass-Butcher "; he is a jail-bird doing the " Rogues'
March to the Island of Elba." An analysis of a few of the
more striking cartoons will serve to close the survey of the
Napoleonic period. " Death and Bonaparte " is a grewsome cartoon by Rowlandson, dated January 1, 1814. Napoleon is seated on a drum with his head clasped between his
hands, staring into the face of a skeleton Death, who is watching the baffled general, face to face. Death mockingly
parodies Napoleon's attitude. A broken eagle, the imperial
standard, lies at his bony feet. In the background the Russian, Prussian, Austrian, and other allied armies are stream-
ing past in unbroken ranks, routing the dismayed legions of
France.

" Bloody Boney, the Corsican Butcher, Left off Trade
and Retiring to Scarecrow Island " is the title of still another
of Rowlandson's characteristic cartoons. In it Napoleon is
represented as riding on a rough-coated donkey and wearing
a fool's cap in place of a crown. His only provision is a
bag of brown bread. His consort is riding on the same
beast, which is being unmercifully flogged with a stick labeled
" Bâton Maréchal."

"THE OVEN OF THE ALLIES."

From an anonymous French cartoon.

Napoleon's escape from Elba was commemorated by Rowlandson in " The Flight of Bonaparte from Hell Bay." In it the foul fiend is amusing himself by letting his captive loose, to work fresh mischief in the world above. He has mounted the Corsican upon a bubble and sends him careering upward back to earth, while hissing dragons pour forth furious blasts to waft the bubble onward.

" Hell Hounds Rallying around the Idol of France " is the

" THE NEW ROBINSON CRUSOE."
From a German caricature.

title of still another of Rowlandson's designs, which appeared in April, 1815. The head and bust of the Emperor drawn on a colossal scale, a hangman's noose around his throat, is mounted on a vast pyramid of human heads, his decapitated victims. Demons are flying through the air to place upon his brow a crown of blazing pitch, while a ring of other excited fiends, whose features represent Maréchal Ney, Lefebre, Davoust and others, with horns, hoofs, and tails, are dancing in triumph around the idol they have replaced. Closely resembling this cartoon of Rowlandson is the German cartoon, which is reproduced in these pages, showing a double-faced

"NAPOLEON CAGED BY THE ALLIES."
From a French cartoon of the period.

Napoleon topping a monument built of skulls. Rowlandson's "Hell Hounds Rallying around the Idol of France" was the last English cartoon directed against Napoleon when he was at the head of France. Two months later the Emperor's power was finally broken at Waterloo.

PART II

FROM WATERLOO THROUGH THE CRIMEAN WAR

CHAPTER VII

AFTER THE DOWNFALL

WITH the downfall of Napoleon the Gillray school of caricature came to an abrupt and very natural close. It was a school born of fear and nurtured upon rancor—a school that indulged freely in obscenity and sacrilege, and did not hesitate to stoop to kick the fallen hero, to heap insult and ignominy upon Napoleon in his exile. Only during a great world crisis, a death struggle of nations, could popular opinion have tolerated such wanton disregard for decency. And when the crisis was passed it came to an end like some malignant growth, strangled by its own virulence. The truth is that Gillray and Rowlandson led caricature into an *impasse;* they deliberately perverted its true function, which is, to advance an argument with the cogent force of a clever orator, to sum up a political issue in terms so simple that a child may read, and not merely to echo back the blatant rancor of the mob. In the hands of a master of the art it becomes an incisive weapon, like the blade with which the matador gives his *coup-de-grace.* Gillray's conception of its office seems to have been that of the red rag to be flapped tauntingly in the face of John Bull; and John Bull obediently bellowed in

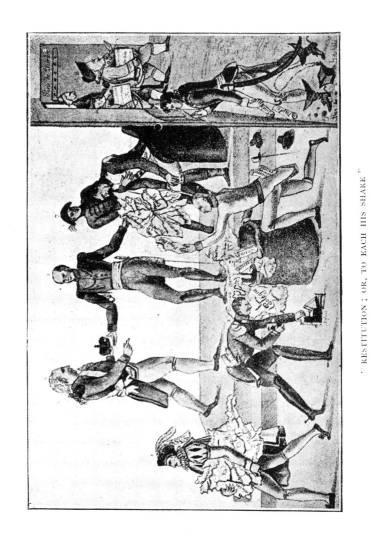

"RESTITUTION ; OR, TO EACH HIS SHARE"

From a colored stamp of the period.

response. It would be idle to deny that for the purpose of spurring on public opinion, the Napoleonic cartoons exercised a potent influence. They kept popular excitement at fever heat; they added fuel to the general hatred. But when the crisis was passed, when the public pulse was beating normally once more, when virulent attacks upon a helpless exile had ceased to seem amusing, there really remained no material upon which caricature of the Gillray type could exercise its offensive ingenuity. What seemed justifiable license when directed against the arch-enemy of European peace would have been insufferable when applied to British statesmen and to the milder problems of local political issues. Another and quite practical reason helps to explain the dearth of political caricature in England for a full generation after the battle of Waterloo, and that is the question of expense. A public which freely gave shillings and even pounds to see its hatred of "Little Boney" interpreted with Gillray's vindictive malice hesitated to expend even pennies for a cartoon on the corn laws or the latest ministerial changes. In England, as well as on the Continent, caricature as an effective factor in politics remained in abeyance until the advent of an essentially modern type of periodical, the comic weekly, of which *La Caricature,* the London *Punch,* the *Fliegende Blätter,* and in this country *Puck* and *Judge,* are the most famous examples. The progress of lithography made such a periodical possible in France as early as 1830, when *La Caricature* was founded by the famous Philipon; but the oppressive laws of censorship throughout Europe prevented any wide development of this class of journalism until after the general political upheaval of 1848.

It would be idle, however, to deny that Gillray exerted a

ADJUSTING THE BALANCE OF POWER AFTER NAPOLEON.

lasting influence upon all future caricature. His license, his
vulgarity, his repulsive perversion of the human face and
form, have found no disciples in later generations; but his
effective assemblage of many figures, the crowded significance
of minor details, the dramatic unity of the whole conception
which he inherited from Hogarth, have been passed on down
the line and still continue to influence the leading cartoonists
of to-day in England, Germany, and the United States,
although to a much less degree in France.   Even at the time
of Napoleon's downfall the few cartoons which appeared in
Paris were far less extreme than their English models, while
the German caricaturists, on the contrary, were extremely
virulent, notably the Berliner, Schadow, who openly acknowledged his indebtedness to the Englishman by signing himself
the Parisian Gillray; and Volz, author of the famous " true
portrait of Napoleon "—a portrait in which Napoleon's face,
upon closer inspection, is seen made up of a head of inextrica-
bly tangled dead bodies, his head surmounted by a bird of
prey, his breast a map of Europe overspread by a vast spider
web, in which the different national capitals are entangled like
so many luckless flies. Had there been more liberty of the
press, an interesting school of political cartoonists might have
arisen at this time in Germany. But they met with such scanty
encouragement that little of real interest is to be gleaned from
this source until after the advent of the Berlin *Kladderadatsch*
in 1848, and the *Fliegende Blätter,* but a short time earlier.

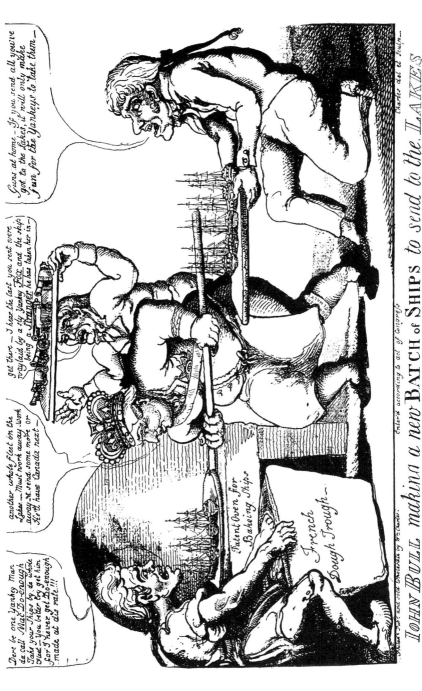

IOHN BULL making a new BATCH of SHIPS to send to the LAKES

This cartoon by William Charles, a Scotchman who was forced to leave Great Britain, and who came to the United States, and wielded his pencil against his renounced country, is in many ways an imitator of Gilray's famous "Tiddy Do, the Great French Gingerbread-Baker, making a new Batch of Kings."

From the collection of the New York Public Library.

Pray Mr Bruin try if you can make up this little Difference between us—The Wasps and Hornets have stung me so hard I wish I had never disturbed their Nests.

I thank you Mr Bruin but I cannot trust the Bull. Tho he has promised to draw in his HORNS he must be safe bound to the Stake before I treat with him.—

Let me unite your hands Madam—Johnny and I have been very friendly since I sent him my Fleet to take care of.

Bruin become MEDIATOR *or* Negociation *for* PEACE.

RUSSIA AS MEDIATOR BETWEEN THE UNITED STATES AND GREAT BRITAIN.
From the collection of the New York Public Library.

AN AMERICAN CARTOON OF THE WAR OF 1812.

A CARICATURE OF THE WAR OF 1812
From the collection of the New York Public Library.

CHAPTER VIII

THE "POIRE"

THROUGHOUT the Napoleonic period England practically had a monopoly in caricature. During the second period, down to the year 1848, France is the center of interest. Prior to 1830, French political cartoons were neither numerous nor especially significant. Indeed they present a simplicity of imagination rather amusing as compared with the complicated English caricatures. A hate of the Jesuits, a mingling of liberalism, touched with Bonapartism, and the war of newspapers furnished the theme. The two symbols constantly recurring are the *girouette*, or weather-cock, and the *éteignoir*, or extinguisher. Many of the French statesmen who played a prominent part during the French Empire and after the Restoration changed their political creed with such surprising rapidity that it was difficult to keep track of their changes. They were accordingly symbolized by a number of weathercocks proportioned to the number of their political conversions, Talleyrand leading the procession, with not less than seven to his credit. The *éteignoir* was constantly used in satire directed against the priesthood, the most famous instance appearing in the *Minerva* in 1819. It took for the text a refrain from a song of Beranger. In this cartoon the Church is personified by the figure of the Pope holding in one hand a sabre, and, in the other, a paper with the words Bulls, crusades, Sicilian vespers, St. Bartholomew. Beside the figure of the Church, torch in hand, is the demon of discord. From the smoke of the torch of the demon various horrors are escaping. We read "the restoration of feudal rights," "feudal privileges," "division of families." Monks are trying to snuff out the memory of Fénelon, Buffon, Voltaire, Rousseau, Montaigne, and other philosophers and thinkers. For ten years the caricaturists played with this theme. A feeble forerunner of *La Caricature,* entitled *Le Nain Jaune,* depended largely for its wit upon the variations it could improvise upon the *girouette* and upon the *éteignoir.*

Yet it would be a mistake to suppose that French art was quite destitute of humorists at the beginning of the century. M. Armand Dayot, in a monograph upon French caricature, mentions among others the names of Isabey, Boilly, and Carle Vernet as rivaling the English cartoonists in the ingenuity of their designs, and surpassing them in artistic finish and harmony of color. "But," he adds, "they were never able to go below the surface in their satire. It would be a mistake to enroll in the hirsute cohort of caricaturists these witty and charming artists, who were more concerned in depicting the pleasures of mundane life than in castigating its vices and irregularities." The 4th of November, 1830, is a momentous date in the history of French caricature. Prior to that time, French cartoons, such as there were, were studiously, even painfully, impersonal. Thackeray, in his delightful essay upon "Caricatures and Lithography," in the "Paris Sketch Book," describes the conditions of this period with the following whimsical allegory:

"As for poor caricature and freedom of the press, they, like the rightful princess in a fairy tale, with the merry fantastic dwarf, her attendant, were entirely in the power of the giant who rules the land. The Princess, the press, was so

THE ORDER OF THE EXTINGUISHERS.

A typical French cartoon of the Restoration.

closely watched and guarded (with some little show, nevertheless, of respect for her rank) that she dared not utter a word of her own thoughts; and, as for poor Caricature, he was gagged and put out of the way altogether."

On this famous 4th of November, however, there appeared the initial number of Philipon's *La Caricature,* which

PROUDHON.

was destined to usher in a new era of comic art, and which proved the most efficacious weapon which the Republicans found to use against Louis Philippe—a weapon as redoubtable as *La Lanterne* of Henri Rochefort became under the Second Empire. Like several of his most famous collaborators, Charles Philipon was a Meridional. He was born in

Lyons at the opening of the century. He studied art in the
atelier of Gros. He married into the family of an eminent
publisher of prints, M. Aubert, and was himself successively the editor of the three most famous comic papers
that France has had, *La Caricature, Charivari*, and the *Jour-*

DIGGING THE GRAVE.

nal pour Rire. The first of these was a weekly paper. The
Charivari appeared daily, and at first its cartoons were almost
exclusively political. Philipon had gathered around him a
group of artists, men like Daumier, Gavarni, Henry Monnier, and Traviès, whose names afterward became famous,
and they united in a veritable crusade of merciless ridicule
against the king, his family, and his supporters. Their satire
took the form of bitter personal attacks, and a very curious
contest ensued between the government and the editorial staff
of the *Charivari*. As Thackeray sums it up, it was a struggle
between "half a dozen poor artists on the one side and His
Majesty Louis Philippe, his august family, and the number-
less placemen and supporters of the monarchy on the other; it
was something like Thersites girding at Ajax." Time after
time were Philipon and his dauntless aids arrested. More
than a dozen times they lost their cause before a jury, yet each
defeat was equivalent to a victory, bringing them new sympathy, and each time they returned to the attack with cartoons

FACSIMILE OF THE FAMOUS DEFENSE PRESENTED BY PHILIPON WHEN ON TRIAL FOR LIBELING THE KING

"Is it my fault, gentlemen of the jury, if his Majesty's face looks like a pear?"

which, if more covert in their meaning, were even more offensive.   Perhaps the most famous of all the cartoons which originated in Philipon's fertile brain is that of the " Pear," which did so much to turn the countenance of Louis Philippe to ridicule—a ridicule which did more than anything else to cause him to be driven from the French throne.   The " Pear " was reproduced in various forms in *La Caricature,* and afterward in *Le Charivari.*   By inferior artists the " Pear " was chalked up on walls all over Paris.   The most politically important of the " Poire " series was produced when Philipon was obliged to appear before a jury to answer for the crime of provoking contempt against the King's person by giving such a ludicrous version of his face.   In his own defense Philipon took up a sheet of paper and drew a large Burgundy pear, in the lower parts round and capacious, narrower near the stalk, and crowned with two or three careless leaves.   " Is there any treason in that? " he asked the jury.   Then he drew a second pear like the first, except that one or two lines were scrawled in the midst of it, which bore somehow an odd resemblance to the features of a celebrated personage; and, lastly, he produced the exact portrait of Louis Philippe; the well-known *toupet,* the ample whiskers—nothing was extenuated or set down maliciously.   " Gentlemen of the jury," said Philipon, " can I help it if His Majesty's face is like a pear? " Thackeray, in giving an account of this amusing trial, makes the curious error of supposing that Philipon's *naïve* defense carried conviction with the jury.   On the contrary, Philipon was condemned and fined, and immediately took vengeance upon the judge and jury by arranging their portraits upon the front page of *Charivari* in the form of a " Pear."   In a hundred different ways his artists rang the changes upon the " pear," and each new attack was the forerunner of a new arrest and trial. One day *La Caricature* published a design representing a gigantic pear surmounting the pedestal in the Place de la Concorde, and bearing the legend, " *Le monument expia-poire.*" This regicidal pleasantry brought Philipon once more into court. " The prosecution sees in this a provocation to murder ! " cried the accused. " It would be at most a provocation to make marmalade." Finally, after a picture of a monkey stealing a pear proved to be an indictable offense, the subject was abandoned as being altogether too expensive a luxury.

CHAPTER IX

B
UT although the " Pear " was forced to disappear, Philipon continued to harass the government, until Louis Philippe, who had gained his crown largely by his championship of the freedom of the press, was driven in desperation to sanction the famous September laws, which virtually strangled its liberty. Yet, in spite of the obstacles thrown in their way, the work of Philipon and of the remarkable corps of satirical geniuses which he gathered round him, forms a pictorial record in which the intimate history of France, from Charles X.'s famous *coup d'état* down to the revolution of 1848, may be read like an open book. The adversaries of the government of 1830 were of two kinds. One kind, of which Admiral Carrel was a type, resorted to passionate argument, to indignant eloquence. The other kind resorted to the methods of the Fronde; they made war by pin-pricks, by bursts of laughter, with all the resources of French gayety and wit. In this method the leading spirit was Philipon, who understood clearly the power that would result from the closest alliance between *la presse et l'image.* Even before *La Caricature* was founded the features of the last of the Bourbons became a familiar subject in cartoons. Invariably the same features are emphasized; a tall, lank figure, frequently contorted like the " india-rubber man " of the dime museums; a narrow, vacuous countenance, a high, receding forehead, over which sparse locks of hair are straggling; a salient jaw, the lips drawn back in a mirthless grin, revealing

THE PIOUS MONARCH.   CARICATURE OF CHARLES X.

huge, ungainly teeth, projecting like the incisors of a horse.
In one memorable cartoon he is expending the full crushing
power of these teeth upon the famous " charter " of 1830,
but is finding it a nut quite too hard to crack.

From the very beginning *La Caricature* assumed an atti-

CHARLES X. IN THE RÔLE OF THE " GREAT
NUTCRACKER."

In this caricature Charles X. is attempting
to break with his teeth a billiard ball on which
is written the word " Charter." The cartoon
is entitled " The Great Nutcracker of July
25th, or the Impotent Horse-jaw " (ganache)—
a play upon words.

tude of hostile suspicion toward Louis Philippe, the pretended
champion of the *bourgeoisie*, whose veneer of expedient republicanism never went deeper than to send his children to the

public schools, and to exhibit himself parading the streets of Paris, umbrella in hand. Two cartoons which appeared in the early days of his reign, and are labeled respectively " *Ne vous y frottez pas* " and " *Il va bon train, le Ministère!* " admirably illustrate the public lack of confidence. The first of these, an eloquent lithograph by Daumier, represents a powerfully built and resolute young journeyman printer standing with hands clinched, ready to defend the liberty of the press. In the background are two groups. In the one Charles X., already worsted in an encounter, lies prone upon the earth; in the other Louis Philippe, waving his ubiquitous umbrella, is with difficulty restrained from assuming the aggressive. The second of these cartoons is more sweeping in its indictment. It represents the sovereign and his ministers in their " chariot of state," one and all lashing the horses into a mad gallop toward a bottomless abyss. General Soult, the Minister of War, is flourishing and snapping a military flag, in place of a whip. At the back of the chariot a Jesuit has succeeded in securing foothold upon the baggage, and is adding his voice to hasten the forward march, all symbolic of the violent momentum of the reactionary movement.

It was not likely that the part which Louis Philippe played in the revolution of 1789, his share in the republican victories of Jemappes and of Valmy, would be forgotten by those who saw in him only a pseudo-republican, a " citizen king " in name only, and who seized eagerly upon the opportunity of mocking at his youthful espousal of republicanism. The names of these battles recur again and again in the caricature of the period, in the legends, in maps conspicuously hung upon the walls of the background. An anonymous cut represents the public gazing eagerly into a magic lantern, the old " Poire " officiating as showman: " You have before you

LOUIS PHILIPPE AT THE FUNERAL OF LAFAYETTE.

"*Enfoncé Lafayette! ... Attrapé, mon vieux!*"

the conqueror of Jemappes and of Valmy. You see him surrounded by his nobles, his generals, and his family, all ready
to die in his defense. See how the jolly rascals fight. They
are not the ones to be driven in disgrace from their kingdom.
Oh, no!" Of all the cartoons touching upon Louis Philippe's
insincerity, probably the most famous is that of Daumier commemorating the death of Lafayette. The persistent popularity of this veteran statesman had steadily become more
and more embarrassing to a government whose reactionary
doctrines he repudiated, and whose political corruption he
despised. "*Enfoncé Lafayette!* . . . *Attrapé, mon
vieux!*" is the legend inscribed beneath what is unquestionably one of the most extraordinary of all the caricatures of
Honoré Daumier. It represents Louis Philippe watching the
funeral cortège of Lafayette, his hands raised to his face in
the pretense of grief, but the face behind distorted into a hideous leer of gratification. M. Arsène Alexandre, in his remarkable work on Daumier, describes this splendid drawing
in the following terms: "Under a grey sky, against the
somber and broken background of a cemetery, rises on a little
hillock the fat and black figure of an undertaker's man. Below him on a winding road is proceeding a long funeral procession. It is the crowd that has thronged to the obsequies of
the illustrious patriot. Through the leafage of the weeping
willows may be seen the white tombstones. The whole scene
bears the mark of a profound sadness, in which the principal
figure seems to join, if one is to judge by his sorrowful attitude and his clasped hands. But look closer. If this undertaker's man, with the features of Louis Philippe, is clasping
his hands, it is simply to rub them together with joy; and
through his fingers, half hiding his countenance, one may
detect a sly grin." The obsequious attitude of the members

THE SHIP OF STATE IN PERIL—ITS SAILORS KNOW NOT TO WHAT SAINTS TO COMMEND THEMSELVES.

of Parliament came in for its share of satirical abuse. " This is not a Chamber, it is a Kennel," is the title of a spirited lithograph by Grandville, representing the French statesmen as a pack of hounds fawning beneath the lash of their imperious keeper, Casimir-Périer. Another characteristic cartoon of Grandville's represents the legislature as an " Infernal laboratory for extracting the quintessence of politics "—a composition which, in its crowded detail, its grim and uncanny suggestiveness, and above all its *bizarre* distortions of the human face and form, shows more plainly than the work of any other French caricaturist the influence of Gillray. A collection of grinning skulls are labeled " Analysis of Human Thought "; state documents of Louis Philippe are being cut and weighed and triturated, while in the foreground a legislator with distended cheeks is wasting an infinite lot of breath upon a blowpipe in his effort to distill the much-sought-for quintessence from a retort filled with fragments of the words " Bonapartism," " anarchy," " equality," " republic," etc. One of the palpable results of the " political quintessence " of Louis Philippe's government took the form of heavy imposts, and these also afforded a subject for Grandville's graphic pencil. " The Public Thrown to the Imposts in the Great Pit of the Budget " first appeared in *La Caricature*. It represented the various taxes under which France was suffering in the guise of strange and unearthly animals congregated in a sort of bear pit, somewhat similar to the one which attracts the attention of all visitors to the city of Berne. The spectacle is one given by the government in power for the amusement of all those connected in any way with public office; in other words, the salaried officials who draw their livelihood from the taxes imposed upon the people. It is for their entertainment that the tax-paying public is being hurled

THE PEOPLE THROWN INTO THE PIT HELD BY THE MONSTERS OF VARIOUS TAXES.

to the monsters below—monsters more uncouth and fantastic than even Mr. H. G. Wells's fertile brain conceived in his " War of the Worlds," or " First Men in the Moon." Daumier in his turn had to have his fling at the ministerial benches of the government of July—the " prostituted Chamber of 1834." At the present day, when the very names of the men whom he attacked are half forgotten, his famous cartoon, " Le Ventre Législatif," is still interesting; yet it is impossible to realize the impression it must have made in the days when every one of those " ventrigoulus," those rotund, somnolent, inanely smiling old men, with the word " *bourgeoisie*" plainly written all over them, were familiar figures in the political world, and Daumier's presentment of them, one and all, a masterly indictment of complacent incapacity. As between Daumier and Grandville, the two leading lights of *La Caricature,* there is little question that the former was the greater. Balzac, who was at one time one of the editors of *La Caricature,* writing under pseudonym of " Comte Alexandre de B.," and was the source of inspiration of one of its leading features, the curious *Etudes de Genre,* once said of Daumier: " *Ce gaillard-là, mes enfants, a du Michel-Ange sous la peau.*" Balzac took Daumier under his protection from the beginning. His first counsel to him was: " If you wish to become a great artist, *faites des dettes!* " Grandville has been defined by later French critics as *un névrose,* a bitter and pessimistic soul. It was he who produced the cruelest compositions that ever appeared in *La Caricature.* He had, however, some admirable pages to his credit, among others his interpretation of Sebastian's famous " L'Ordre règne à Varsovie." Fearfully sinister is the field of carnage, with the Cossack, with bloody *pique,* mounting guard, smoking his pipe tranquilly, on his face the horrible expression

" Once more, Madame, do you wish divorce, or do you not wish divorce ? You are perfectly free to choose ?"

of satisfaction over a work well done. Grandville also conceived the idea, worthy of a great cartoonist, of Processions
and Cortèges. These enabled him to have pass before the
eye, under costumes, each conveying some subtle irony or
allusion, all the political men in favor. Every occasion was

THE RESUSCITATION OF THE FRENCH CENSORSHIP.
By Grandville.

good. A religious procession, and the men of the day appeared as choir boys, as acolytes, etc. *Un vote de budget,*
and then it was *une marche de boeuf gras,* with savages,
musketeers, clowns forming the escort of "*M. Gros, gras
et bête.*" It is easy to guess who was the personage so desig-

LOUIS PHILIPPE AS BLUEBEARD

"Sister Press, do you see anything?" "Sister Press, do you see anything?"
"Nothing, but the July sun beating on the "Two Cavaliers, urging their horses across
dusty road." the plain, and bearing a banner."

nated. Nothing is more amusing than these pages, full of a
verve, soutenue de pince sans rire.

It is one of the many little ironies of Louis Philippe's
reign that, after having owed his election to his supposed
advocacy of freedom of the press, he should in less than two
years take vigorous measures to stifle it. Some of the best
known cartoons that appeared in *La Caricature* deal with this
very subject. One of these, which bears the signature of
Grandville and is marked by all the vindictive bitterness of
which that artist was the master, represents Louis Philippe
in the rôle of Bluebeard, who, dagger in hand, is about to
slay his latest wife. The wife, the " Constitution," lies
prostrate, bound with thongs. The corpses of this political
Bluebeard's other victims may be seen through the open door
of the secret chamber. Leaning over the balcony and scan-
ning the horizon is the figure of Sister Anne, in this case
symbolic of the Press. The unfortunate " Constitution,"
feeling that her last minute has come, calls out: " Sister
Press, do you see nothing coming?" The Press replies:
" I see only the sun of July beating down, powdering the
dusty road and parching the green fields." Again the Constitution cries: " Sister Press, do you see nothing coming?" And this time the Press calls back: " I see two
cavaliers urging their horses across the plain and carrying a
banner." Below the castle of Bluebeard may be seen the
figures of the two cavaliers. The banner which they carry
bears the significant word, " Republic! "

Another cartoon bearing upon the same subject represents
Liberty wearing a Phrygian cap, driving the chariot of the
sun. The King and his ministers and judges, above whom a
crow hovers ominously, flapping its black wings, are seeking
to stop the course of liberty by thrusting between the spokes

of the wheels sticks and rods inscribed " Lawsuits against the Press," while Talleyrand comes to their aid by throwing beneath the wheels stones symbolizing " standing armies," " imposts," " holy alliance," and so forth.   This cartoon is inscribed: " It would be easier to stop the course of the sun," and is the work of Traviès, who is best known as the creator of the grotesque hunchback figure, " Mayeux."

BARBARISM AND THE CHOLERA INVADING EUROPE IN 1831.

RAID ON THE WORKSHOP OF THE LIBERTY OF THE PRESS.

CHAPTER X

A PECULIAR feature of French caricature, especially after political subjects were largely forbidden, was the creation of certain famous types who soon became familiar to the French public, and whose reappearances from day to day in new and ever grotesque situations were hailed with growing delight. Such were the Mayeux of Traviès and the Macaire and Bertrand of Daumier, who in course of time became as celebrated, in a certain sense, as the heroes of "The Three Musketeers." In his "Curiosités Esthétiques" Beaudelaire has told the story of the origin of Mayeux. "There was," he says, "in Paris a sort of clown named Le Claire, who had the run of various low resorts and theaters. His specialty was to make *têtes d'expression,* that is, by a series of facial contortions he would express successively the various human passions. This man, a clown by nature, was very melancholy and possessed with a mad desire for friendship. All the time not occupied in practice and in giving his grotesque performances he spent in searching for a friend, and when he had been drinking, tears of solitude flowed freely from his eyes. Traviès saw him. It was a time when the great patriotic enthusiasm of July was still at its height. A luminous idea entered his brain. Mayeux was created, and for a long time afterward this same turbulent Mayeux talked, screamed, harangued, and gesticulated in the memory of the people of Paris."

In a hundred different guises, in the blue blouse of the

workman, the apron of the butcher, the magisterial gown of judge or advocate, this hunchback Mayeux, this misshapen parody upon humanity, endeared himself to the Parisian public. Virulent, salacious, corrupt, he was a sort of French Mr. Hyde—the shadow of secret weaknesses and vices, lurk-

TRAVIÈS'S " MAYEUX."

" Adam destroyed us by the apple ; Lafayette by the pear."

ing behind the Dr. Jekyll of smug *bourgeois* respectability; and the French public recognized him as a true picture of their baser selves. They laughed indulgently over the broad, Rabelaisian jests that unfailingly accompanied each new cartoon—jests which M. Dayot has admirably characterized as " seasoned with coarse salt, more German than Gallic, and forming a series of legends which might be made into a veritable catechism of pornography." This Mayeux series is not, strictly speaking, political in its essence. It touches upon all sides of life, without discrimination and without respect. It even trespasses upon the subject of that forbidden fruit, " Le Poire." In an oft-cited cartoon, Mayeux with extended arms, his head sunken lower than usual between his huddled shoulders, is declaiming : " Adam destroyed us with the apple; Lafayette has destroyed us with the pear! " And later, when repeated arrests, verdicts, fines, edicts had banished politics from the arena of caricature, Mayeux was still a privileged character. Like Chicot, the jester, who could speak his mind fearlessly to his " Henriquet," while the ordinary courtier cringed obsequiously, Mayeux shared the proverbial privilege of children and buffoons, to speak the truth. And oftentimes it was not even necessary for his creator, Traviès, to manifest any overt political significance; the public were always more than ready to look for it below the surface. In such a picture as that of Mayeux, in Napoleonic garb striking an attitude before a portrait of the Little Corporal and exclaiming, " *Comme je lui ressemble!* " they inevitably discovered a hint that there were other hypocrites more august than Mayeux who fancied themselves worthy of filling Napoleon's shoes.

Even more famous than Mayeux are the Macaire and Bertrand series, the joint invention of Philipon, who supplied the ideas and the text, and of Daumier, who executed the designs. According to Thackeray, whose analysis of these masterpieces of French caricature has become classic, they had their origin in an old play, the "Auberge des Adrets," in which

Messieurs Macaire and Bertrand have found it expedient to make a hurried departure for Belgium for the purpose of evading French justice. The eloquent Macaire, on reaching the frontier, declaims as follows; "Hail to thee, O land of hospitality! Hail, fatherland of those who haven't got any! Sacred refuge of all unfortunates proscribed by human justice, hail! To all drooping hearts Belgium is dear."

two thieves escaped from the galleys were introduced, Robert
Macaire, the clever rogue, and Bertrand, his friend, the
" butt and scapegoat on all occasions of danger." The play
had been half-forgotten when it was revived by a popular and
clever actor, Frederick Lemaître, who used it as a vehicle for
political burlesque. The play was suppressed, but *Le Charivari* eagerly seized upon the idea and continued it from day to

EXTINGUISHED !

day in the form of a pictorial puppet show, of which the public never seemed to weary. Thackeray's summary of the
characters of these two illustrious rascals can scarcely be improved upon:

" M. Robert Macaire [he says] is a compound of Fielding's ' Blueskin ' and Goldsmith's ' Beau Tibbs.' He has the
dirt and dandyism of the one, with the ferocity of the other:
sometimes he is made to swindle, but where he can get a

shilling more, M. Macaire will murder without scruple; he performs one and the other act (or any in the scale between them) with a similar bland imperturbability, and accompanies his actions with such philosophical remarks as may be expected from a person of his talents, his energies, his amiable life and character. Bertrand is the simple recipient of Macaire's jokes, and makes vicarious atonement for his crimes, acting, in fact, the part which pantaloon performs in

LOUIS PHILIPPE AS CAIN WITH THE ANGELS OF
JUSTICE IN PURSUIT.

the pantomime, who is entirely under the fatal influence of clown. He is quite as much a rogue as that gentleman, but he has not his genius and courage. . . Thus Robert Macaire and his companion Bertrand are made to go through the world; both swindlers, but the one more accomplished than the other. Both robbing all the world, and Robert robbing his friend, and, in the event of danger, leaving him faithfully in the lurch. There is, in the two characters, some grotesque good for the spectator—a kind of 'Beggars' Opera' moral. . . And with these two types of clever and stupid knavery, M. Philipon and his companion Daumier have created a world of pleasant satire upon all the prevailing abuses of the day."

The Macaire and Bertrand series were less directly political in their scope than that of Travies's hunchback; at least, their political allusions were more carefully veiled. Yet the first of the series had portrayed in Macaire's picturesque green coat and patched red trousers no less a personage than the old " Poire " himself, and the public remembered it. When politics were banished from journalism they persisted in finding in each new escapade of Macaire and Bertrand an

LAUGHING JOHN—CRYING JOHN.
July, 1830.   February, 1848.

allusion to some fresh scandal, if not connected with the King himself, at least well up in the ranks of governmental hypocrites. And, although the specific scandals upon which they are based, the joint-stock schemes for floating worthless enterprises, the thousand-and-one plausible humbugs of the period, are now forgotten, to those who take the trouble to read between the lines, these masterpieces of Daumier's genius form a luminous exposition of the *morale* of the government and the court circles.

CHAPTER XI

IN contrast with the brilliancy of the French artists, the work in England during these years, at least prior to the establishment of *Punch,* is distinctly disappointing. The one man who might have raised caricature to an even higher level than that of Gillray and Rowlandson was George Cruikshank, but he withdrew early in life from political caricature, preferring, like Hogarth, to concentrate his talent upon the dramatic aspects of contemporary social life. Yet at the outset of his career, just as he was coming of age, Cruikshank produced one cartoon that has remained famous because it anticipated by thirty years the attitude of Mill and Cobden in 1846. It was in 1815, just after the battle of Waterloo had secured an era of peace for Europe, that he produced his protest against the laws restricting the importation of grain into England. He called it " The Blessings of Peace; or, the Curse of the Corn Bill." A cargo of foreign grain has just arrived and is being offered for sale by the supercargo: " Here is the best for fifty shillings." On the shore a group of British landholders wave the foreigner away: " We won't have it at any price. We are determined to keep up our own to eighty shillings, and if the poor can't buy it at that price, why, they must starve." In the background a storehouse with tight-shut doors bulges with home-grown grain. A starving family stand watching while the foreign grain is thrown overboard, and the father says: " No, no, masters, I'll not starve, but quit my native

97

land, where the poor are crushed by those they labor to support, and retire to one more hospitable, and where the arts
of the rich do not interpose to defeat the providence of God."

After Cruikshank, until the advent of the men who made
Punch famous,—Richard Doyle, John Leech, John Tenniel,
and their successors,—there are no cartoonists in England
whose work rises above mediocrity. When the death of
Canning brought Wellington and Peel into power, a series of
colored prints bearing the signature H. Heath, and persist-
ently lampooning the new ministry, enjoyed a certain vogue.
They scarcely rose above the level of the penny comic valen-
tine, which they much resembled in crudeness of color and
poverty of invention. One set, entitled " Our Theatrical
Celebrities," depicted the Premier as stage manager, the
other members of the cabinet as leading man, première
danseuse, prompter, etc. Another series depicts the same
statesmen as so many thoroughbreds, to be auctioned off to the
highest bidder, and describes the good points of each in the
most approved language of the turf. Lot No. 1 is the Duke
of Wellington, described as " the famous charger, Arthur ";
Lot No. 2 is Peel, the " Good Old Cobb, Bobby," and the
rest of the series continue the same vein of inane witticism.
Somewhat more point is to be found in the portrayal of Wellington buried up to his neck in his own boot—one of the
universal Wellington boots of the period. The cartoonist's
thought, quite obviously, was that the illustrious hero of
Waterloo had won his fame primarily in boots and spurs,
and that as a statesman he became a very much shrunken and
insignificant figure. In its underlying thought this cartoon
suggests comparison with the familiar " Grandpa's Hat "
cartoons of the recent Harrison administration. Very rarely
Heath broke away from home politics and touched upon in-

ternational questions of the day. A print showing the
Premier engaged in the task of " making a rushlight," which
he is just withdrawing cautiously from a large tub labeled
" Greece," is an allusion to the part played by Great Britain

A WELLINGTON BOOT
or the Head of the Armye

THE DUKE OF WELLINGTON IN CARICATURE
From the collection of the New York Public Library.

in helping to add the modest light of Greek independence to
the general illumination of civilized Europe.

Another man whose work enjoyed a long period of shop-
window popularity, and who nevertheless did not always rise
above the comic-valentine level, was John Doyle, who owes
his memory less to his own work than to the fact that he was
the father of a real master of the art, Richard Doyle. Parton, in his history of " Caricature and Other Comic Art,"

notes the elder Doyle's remarkable prolificness, estimating his collected prints at upward of nine hundred; and he continues: " It was a custom with English print-sellers to keep portfolios of his innocent and amusing pictures to let out by the evening to families about to engage in the arduous work of entertaining their friends at dinner.   He excelled greatly in his portraits, many of which, it is said by contemporaries, are the best ever taken of the noted men of that day, and may safely be accepted as historical.   Brougham, Peel, O'Connell, Hume, Russell, Palmerston, and others appear in his works as they were in their prime, with little distortion or exaggeration, the humor of the pictures being in the situation portrayed.   Thus, after a debate in which allusion was made to an ancient egg anecdote, Doyle produced a caricature in which the leaders of parties were drawn as hens sitting upon eggs.   The whole interest of the picture lies in the speaking likeness of the men."

CHAPTER XII

W HAT the advent of *La Caricature* did for French comic art was done for England by the birth of *Punch,* the " London Charivari," on July 17, 1841. It is not surprising that this veteran organ of wit and satire, essentially British though it is in the quality and range of its humor, should have inspired a number of different writers successively to record its annals. Mr. M. H. Spielmann, whose admirable volume is likely to remain the authoritative history, points out that the very term " cartoon " in its modern sense is in reality a creation of *Punch's.* In the reign of Charles I., he says, the approved phrase was, " a mad designe "; in the time of George II. it was known as a " hieroglyphic "; throughout the golden age of Gillray and Cruikshank " caricature " was the epithet applied to the separate copperplate broadsides displayed in the famous shops of Ackermann, Mrs. Humphrey, and McClean. But it was not until July, 1843, when the first great exhibition of cartoons for the Houses of Parliament was held—gigantic designs handling the loftiest subjects in the most elevated artistic spirit—that *Punch* inaugurated his own sarcastic series of " cartoons," and by doing so permanently enriched the language with a new word, or rather with new meaning for an old word. *Punch,* however, did far more than merely to change the terminology of caricature; he revolutionized its spirit; he made it possible for Gladstone to say of it that " in his early days, when an artist was engaged to produce political

satires, he nearly always descended to gross personal caricature, and sometimes to indecency. To-day the humorous
press showed a total absence of vulgarity and a fairer treatment, which made this department of warfare always
pleasing."

As in the case of other famous characters of history, the
origin and parentage of *Punch* have been much disputed, and
a variety of legends have grown up about the source of its
very name, the credit for its genesis being variously assigned
to its original editors, Henry Mayhew, Mark Lemon, the
printer Joseph Last, the writer Douglas Jerrold, and a
number of obscurer literary lights. One story cited by Mr.
Spielmann, although clearly apocryphal, is nevertheless
worthy of repetition. According to this story, somebody at
one of the preliminary meetings spoke of the forthcoming
paper as being like a good mixture of punch, good for nothing
without Lemon, when Mayhew caught up the idea and cried,
" A capital idea ! We'll call it *Punch!* "

In marked contrast to its French prototype, the " London
Charivari " was from the beginning a moderate organ, and a
stanch supporter of the Crown. In its original prospectus
its political creed was outlined as follows: " *Punch* has no
party prejudices; he is conservative in his opposition to
Fantoccini and political puppets, but a progressive whig in his
love of *small change* and a repeal of the union with public
Judies." And to this day this policy of " hitting all
around," of avoiding any bitter and prolonged partisanship,
is the keynote of *Punch's* popularity and prestige. How this
attitude has been consistently maintained in its practical working is well brought out by Mr. Spielmann in his chapter
dedicated to the periodic *Punch* dinners, where the editorial
councils have always taken place:

" When the meal is done and cigars and pipes are duly
lighted, subjects are deliberately proposed in half a dozen
quarters, until quite a number may be before the Staff.   They

THE LAND OF LIBERTY.

are fought all round the Table, and unless obviously and
strikingly good, are probably rejected or attacked with good-
humored ridicule or withering scorn. . . And when the subject of a cartoon is a political one, the debate grows hot and
the fun more furious, and it usually ends by Tories and

Radicals accepting a compromise, for the parties are pretty evenly balanced at the Table; while Mr. Burnand assails both sides with perfect indifference.   At last, when the intellectual tug-of-war, lasting usually from half-past eight for just an

"*WHAT? YOU YOUNG YANKEE-NOODLE, STRIKE YOUR OWN FATHER!*"

hour and three-quarters by the clock, is brought to a conclusion, the cartoon in all its details is discussed and determined; and then comes the fight over the title and the 'cackle,' amid all the good-natured chaff and banter of a pack of boisterous, high-spirited schoolboys."

Down to the close of the period covered in the present
chapter, the cartoon played a relatively small part in the
weekly contents of *Punch,* averaging barely one a week, and

LOUIS PHILIPPE AS " THE NAPOLEON OF PEACE."
From the collection of the New York Public Library.

being omitted altogether from many numbers.   During these
years the dominating spirit was unquestionably John Leech,
who produced no less than two hundred and twenty-three
cartoons out of a total of three hundred and fourteen, or more

than twice as many as all the other contributors put together. He first appeared with a pageful of " Foreign Affairs " in the fourth issue of *Punch*—a picture of some huddled groups of foreign refugees—a design remembered chiefly because it for the first time introduced to the world the artist's sign-manual, a leech wriggling in a water bottle.

Of Doyle's political plates during these early years, none is more interesting to the American reader than the few rare occasions upon which he seeks to express the British impression of the United States. One of these, " The Land of Liberty," appeared in 1847. A lean and lanky, but beardless, Uncle Sam tilts lazily back in his rocking-chair, a six-shooter in his hand, a huge cigar between his teeth. One foot rests carelessly upon a bust of Washington, which he has kicked over. The other is flung over the back of another chair in sprawling insolence. In the ascending clouds of smoke appear the Stars and Stripes, surrounded by a panorama of outrages, duels, barroom broils, lynch law, etc., and above them all, the contending armies of the Mexican war, over whom a gigantic devil hovers, his hands extended in a malignant benediction. A closely analogous cartoon of this same year by Richard Doyle sharply satirized Louis Philippe as the " Napoleon of Peace," and depicted in detail the unsatisfactory condition of European affairs as seen from the British vantage ground. As a consequence of this cartoon *Punch* was for some time excluded from Paris.

From 1848 onward the cartoons in *Punch* look upon the world politics from a constantly widening angle. Indeed, the same remark holds good for the comic organs not only of England, but of France, Germany, Italy, and the other leading nations as well. Throughout the second half of the nineteenth century the international relations of the leading

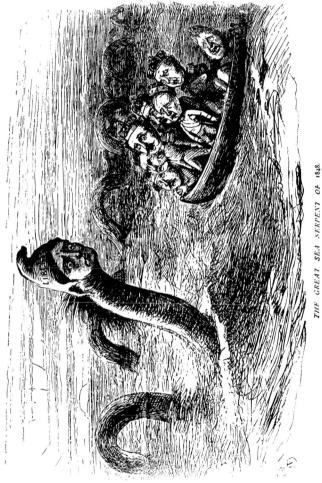

THE GREAT SEA SERPENT OF 1848.

From the collection of the New York Public Library.

powers may be followed almost without a break in the cartoons of *Punch* and *Judy*, of the *Fliegende Blätter* and the *Kladderadatsch*, of *Don Pirlone*, of the *Journal pour Rire*, of *Life* and *Puck* and *Judge*, and the countless host of their followers and imitators.

A BIRD'S-EYE VIEW OF EUROPE IN 1830.

From the collection of the New York Public Library.

CHAPTER XIII

RETROSPECTIVE

THE close of the first half of the nineteenth century marks a convenient moment for a backward glance. These fifty years, which began with the consulship of the first Napoleon and closed on the eve of the third Napoleon's *coup d'état,* witnessed the rise and fall of more than one Napoleonic spirit in the realm of comic art. It was essentially a period of individualism, of the one-man power in caricature. Existing conditions forbade a logical and unbroken development of the political cartoon; it evolved only by fits and starts. It was often less an expression of the popular mood than a vehicle for personal enthusiasm or personal rancor; at the hands of just a few masters, it verged upon the despotic. At intervals, first in one country and then in another, a Gillray, a Rowlandson, a Daumier, would blaze forth, brilliant, erratic, meteor-like, leaving behind them a trail of scintillating suggestion, destined to fire some new fuse, to start caricature along some new curve of eccentricity. The importance of these fifty years, the lasting influence of these forerunners of the modern cartoonists, must not be underrated. Without the inspiration of their brilliant successes, and, it may also be added, the useful lessons of their errors and failures, the cartoon of to-day would be radically different, and probably greatly inferior to what it is. Above all, they taught, by two tremendous object lessons, the potent force that lies in pictorial satire—by the share which English cartoonists had in the overthrow of Napoleon I., and which

French cartoonists had in the downfall of Louis Philippe. But it was only with the advent of the modern comic weekly of the high type represented by *Punch* that it became possible to develop schools of caricature with definite aims and es-

DAUMIER

Caricatured by Benjamin.

Daumier fut le peintre ordinaire
Des pairs, des députés et des Robert-Macaire.
Son rude crayon fait l'histoire de nos jours.
—O l'étonnante boule ! ô la bonne figure !
—Je le crois pardieu bien, car Daumier est
    toujours Excellent en caricature.

tablished traditions—schools that have tended steadily to eliminate and reject the old-time elements of vulgarity and exaggeration, to gain the increased influence that comes from sobriety of method and higher artistic excellence, and to hold erratic individuality in check. Few people who are not

directly concerned in its making ever realize how essentially
the modern caricature is a composite production. Take, for
example, the big, double-page cartoon which has become such
a familiar weekly feature in *Puck* or *Judge*, with its complicated group of figures, its suggestive background, its mul-
titude of clever minor points; the germ idea has been picked
out from perhaps a dozen others, as the result of careful
deliberation, and from this starting point the whole design
has been built up, detail by detail, representing the joint
cleverness of the entire editorial staff.   But the collaboration
reaches further back than this.   A political cartoon resembles
in a way a composite photograph, which embodies not merely
the superimposed features of the men who sat before the
camera, but something also of the countless generations before
them, who have made their features what they are by trans-
mitting from father to son something of their own
personality.   In the same way, the political cartoon of to-
day is the product of a gradual evolution, mirroring back the
familiar features of many a cartoon of the past.   It is not
merely an embodiment of the ideas of the satirists who suggested it and the artist who drew it, but also of many a traditional and stereotyped symbol, bequeathed from generation
to generation by artists dead and gone.   The very essence
of pictorial satire, its alpha and omega, so to speak, is sym-
bolism, the use of certain established types, conventional
personifications of Peace and War, Death and Famine and
Disease, Father Time with his scythe, the Old Year and the
New; the Russian Bear, the British Lion, and the American
Eagle; Uncle Sam and Columbia, Britannia and John Bull.
These figures, as we have them to-day, cannot point to any
one creator.   They are not an inspiration of the moment,
a stroke of genius, like Daumier's " Macaire " or Traviès's

" Mayeux." They are the product of a century of evolution, a gradual survival of the fittest, resulting from the unconscious natural selection of popular approval. No better specific instance can be taken than that of the familiar figure of John Bull as he appears from week to week in the contemporary pages of *Punch,* for his descent may be traced in an unbroken line—there are no missing links. No single British caricaturist, from Gillray to Du Maurier, can claim the credit for having invented him; yet each in his turn has contributed something, a touch here, a line there, toward making him what he is to-day. As Mr. Spielmann has pointed out, the earliest prototype of *Punch's* John Bull is to be sought in Gillray's conception of " Farmer George," that figured in a long series of malevolent caricatures depicting George III., as a gaping country lout, a heavy, dull-witted yokel. There is no more curious paradox in the history of caricature than that this figure of " Farmer George," conceived in pure malice as a means of inspiring resentment against a king popularly believed to care more for his farmyard than for the interests of his subjects, should by gradual transition have come to be accepted as the symbolic figure of the nation. Yet the successive steps are easy enough to understand. When Gillray's point of attack had shifted from the throne of England to the throne of France, his type of " Farmer George " needed but slight modification to become a huge, ungainly ogre, the incarnation of British wrath against " Little Boney "—shaking a formidable fist at the coast of Calais, wading knee-deep across the channel, or greedily opening a cavernous jaw to take in a soul-satisfying meal of French frigates. But beneath the exaggerated ferocity of Gillray's extreme type, the idea of a farmer as the national figure is never quite lost sight of. In Gillray's later

JOHN LEECH (1857)

JAMES GILLRAY (1802).

JOHN PHILLIPS (1829)

G CRUIKSHANK (1829)

MR. JOHN BULL AT HOME.
SIR JOHN TENNIEL IN "PUNCH" (1856).

1901

JAMES GILLRAY (1795)

JOHN BULL AT HOME.—JAMES GILLRAY (1790).

THOMAS ROWLANDSON (1793)

THE EVOLUTION OF JOHN BULL.

cartoons the conception of John Bull had already taken on a more consistent and definite form. At the hands of Rowlandson and Woodward he lost much of his uncouthness and began to assume a mellower and more benignant aspect; a cartoon by the latter, entitled " Genial Rays," pictures him reclining luxuriously upon a bed of roses, basking in " the sun

HENRI MONNIER IN THE ROLE OF JOSEPH PRUD-
HOMME.
" Never shall my daughter become the wife of
a scribbler."
By Daumier

of patriotism," the image of agricultural contentment. A certain coarseness and vulgarity, however, clung to him until well down into the forties, when the refining touch of Leech and Tenniel gradually idealized him into the portly, choleric, well-to-do rural gentleman who is to-day such a familiar figure the world over. This type of John Bull as the representative Briton once called forth some thoroughly characteristic comments from John Ruskin. "Is it not surely," he asks, "some overruling power in the nature of things, quite other than the desire of his readers, which compels Mr. Punch, when the squire, the colonel, and the admiral are to be at once expressed, together with all that they legislate or fight for, in the symbolic figure of the nation, to present the incarnate Mr. Bull always as a farmer—never as a manufacturer or shopkeeper?" Such a view on the part of Mr. Ruskin is consistent with his life-long insistence upon literal truth in art. But he was obviously mistaken when he questioned that John Bull is the deliberate choice of the British public. The average Englishman, whether soldier or sailor, statesman, merchant, or manufacturer, approves and enjoys the pleasant fiction that the representative type is a good, old-fashioned country gentleman, conservative and rather insular, a supporter of landed interests, a patron of country sports; in short, one who lives his life close to his native soil, who seems to personify the rolling down, the close-clipped hedge, the trim gardenplot, the neat thatched roof, things which typify England the world over.

Not only are most of the accepted symbolic figures—John Bull, Uncle Sam, and the rest—what they are because they meet with popular approval, but no cartoonist to-day could venture upon any radical departure from the established type—a bearded John Bull, a smooth-shaven Uncle Sam—without calling down public disfavor upon his head. If one stops to think of it, our own accepted national type, the tall, lank, awkward figure, the thin, angular Yankee face with a shrewd and kindly twinkle in the eye, is even less representative of the average American than John Bull is of the average Briton. It is interesting to recall that before the Civil War our national type frequently took the form of a Southerner—regularly in the pages of *Punch*.   To-day, in England and in America, there is but one type of Uncle Sam, and we would not tolerate a change.   It may be that in the gaunt, loose-knit frame, the strong and rugged features we recognize a kinship to that sterling and essentially American type of man which found its best exponent in Lincoln, and that this is the reason why Uncle Sam has become the most universally accepted and the best beloved of all our conventional types.

CHAPTER XIV

'48 AND THE COUP D'ÉTAT

IT was only natural that caricature, like every other form of free expression of opinion, should feel the consequences of the general political upheaval of 1848; and these consequences differed widely in the different countries of Europe, according to the degree of civic liberty which that revolutionary movement had effected. In Germany, for example, it resulted in the establishment of a whole group of comic weeklies, with a license for touching upon political topics quite unprecedented in that land of imperialism and censorship. In France, on the contrary, political caricature came to an abrupt close just at a time when it had begun to give promise of exceptional interest. Louis Napoleon, who owed his elevation to the presidency of the republic chiefly to the popular belief in his absolute harmlessness, developed a most unexpected and disconcerting strength of character. His capacity for cunning and unscrupulousness was yet to be learned; but a feeling of distrust was already in the air, and the caricaturists were quick to reflect it. Louis Napoleon, however, was keenly alive to the deadly harm wrought to his predecessor by Philipon's pictorial sharp-shooters, and he did not propose to let history repeat itself by holding him up to public ridicule, after the fashion of the poor old " Poire," the citizen king. Accordingly the *coup d'état* was hardly an accomplished fact when press laws were passed of such a stringent nature that the public press, and pictorial satire along with it, was reduced to a state of vassalage, dependent upon the imperial caprice, a condition that lasted upward of fifteen years. Consequently, the few cartoons satirizing Napoleon III., that emanate from French sources, either belong to the closing years of his reign or else antedate the law of 1851, which denied trial by jury to all cases of infringement of the press laws. The latter cartoons, however, are of special interest, for they serve to throw important light upon the popular state of mind just prior to the famous *coup d'état.*

The majority of these cartoons appeared in the pages of *Charivari,* and some of the best are due to the caustic pencil

" THE ONLY LAMPS AUTHORIZED TO LIGHT THE
PATH OF THE GOVERNMENT "
By Vernier in " Charivari."

of Charles Vernier. A good specimen of this artist's work is a lithograph entitled " The Only Lamps Authorized for the Present to Light up the Path of the Government," showing Louis Napoleon marching along sedately, his hands clasped behind his back and his way illuminated by three

lantern-bearers. The lanterns are, respectively, *La Patrie
du Soir, Le Moniteur du Soir* and *La Gazette de France,*
newspapers then in favor with the government.   Just in front
of Louis Napoleon, however, may be seen a dark and
ominous manhole.   Another of Vernier's cartoons is called

AN ITALIAN CARTOON OF '48.

" The Shooting Match in the Champs Elysées."   The target
is the head of the Constitution surmounting a pole.   Napoleon is directing the efforts of the contestants.   " The man
who knocks the target over completely," he is saying, " I will
make my Prime Minister."   The contrast between the great
Napoleon and the man whom Victor Hugo liked so to call
" Napoleon the Little " suggested another pictorial effort of
Vernier.   A veteran of the Grand Army is watching the
coach of the state passing by, Napoleon holding the reins.
" What!   That my Emperor! " exclaims the veteran, shad-
ing his eyes.   " Those rascally Englishmen, how they have
changed my vision! "   The methods by which Louis Napoleon obtained his election first as President for ten years, and
secondly as Emperor of the French, were satirized in *Charivari* by Daumier in a cartoon called " Les Aveugles " (The
Blind).   In the center of this cartoon is a huge ballot jar

marked "Universal Suffrage." Around this the sightless voters are laboriously groping.

Many were the designs by which Daumier in *Charivari* satirized Louis Napoleon's flirtation with the French republic. In one of them the Prince, bearing a remote resemblance in manner and in dress to Robert Macaire, is offering the lady his arm. "*Belle dame*," he is saying, "will you accept my escort?" To which she replies coldly: "Monsieur, your

NAPOLEON LE PETIT.
By Vernier.

passion is entirely too sudden. I can place no great faith in it."

Pictorial expressions of opinion regarding the "great crime" of 1851, which once more replaced a republic with an empire, must be sought for outside of France. But there was one subject at this time upon which even the strictest of edicts could not enforce silence, and that was the subject of Napoleon's marriage to Eugénie. The Emperor's Spanish

bride was never popular, not even during the first years of the
Second Empire, before she began to meddle with affairs of
state; and in many incisive ways the Parisians heaped ridicule
upon her.   A curious little pamphlet, with text and illustra-
tions, about the new Empress was sold in Paris at the time of
the marriage.   This pamphlet was entirely complimentary
and harmless.   The biting humor of it was on the title-page,
which the vendors went about crying in the streets: " The

THE NEW SIAMESE TWINS.

portrait and virtues of the Empress, all for two sous! "   But
for a frank expression of what the world thought of the new
master of the destinies of France, it is necessary to turn to the
contemporary pages of *Punch*.   The " London Charivari "
was at this time just entering upon its most glorious epoch of
political caricature.   John Leech, one of the two great
English cartoonists of the past half century, had arrived at
the maturity of his talent; the second, John Tenniel, was
destined soon to join the staff of *Punch* in place of Richard
Doyle, who resigned in protest against the editorial policy of
attacking the Roman Catholic Church.   Both of these artists
possessed a technical skill and a degree of artistic inspiration
that raised them far above the level of the mere caricaturist.

And as it happened, the world was entering upon a long succession of stormy scenes, destined to furnish them with matter worthy of their pencils. After forty years of peace,

LOUIS NAPOLEON AND MADAME FRANCE.

Europe was about to incur an epidemic of war. The clash between Turkey and Russia in 1853 was destined to assume international proportions in the Crimean War; England's troubles were to be augmented by the revolt of her Indian mercenaries; the Russian war was to be closely followed by another between France and Austria; by the enfranchisement of Italy from the Alps to the Adriatic; the bitter struggle between Prussia and Austria; and the breaking up of the Confederation of the Rhine, with the Franco-Prussian War looming up in the near future. It was on the threshold of such troublous times, and as if prophetic of the end of European tranquillity, that Leech signalized the accession of Napoleon III. as Emperor with the significant cartoon,

" France is Tranquil! ! !" Poor France cannot well be
otherwise than tranquil, for Mr. Leech depicts her bound
hand and foot, a chain-shot fastened to her feet and a sentry
standing guard over her with a bayonet. The artist soon
followed this up with another cartoon, evidently suggested
by the initial plate of Hogarth's famous series of " The
Rake's Progress." The Prince President, in the character of
the Rake, has just come into his inheritance, and has cast aside

LOUIS NAPOLEON'S PROCLAMATION.
By Gill.

his former mistress, Liberté, to whom he is offering money,
her mother (France) standing by, an indignant witness to the
scene. His military tailor is measuring him for a new
imperial uniform, while behind him a priest (in allusion to the

financial aid which the Papal party was receiving from Napoleon) is helping himself from a plate of money standing beside the President.   On the floor is a confused litter of swords, knapsacks, bayonets, crowns, crosses of the Legion of

SPLIT CROW IN THE CRIMEA.
From Punch.

Honor, the Code Napoléon, and other miscellaneous reminders of Louis' well-known craze on the subject of his uncle and his uncle's ideas.   Mr. Tenniel's early cartoons of Louis Napoleon are scarcely more kindly.   The Emperor's approaching marriage is hit off in one entitled " The Eagle in Love," in which Eugénie, represented with the most unflattering likeness, is employed in paring the imperial eagle's talons. In 1853 Tenniel depicts an " International Poultry Show," where we see among the entries a variety of eagles—the

Prussian eagle, the American eagle, the two-headed Russian and Austrian eagles—and among them a wretched mongrel, more closely akin to a bedraggled barn-door fowl than to the "French Eagle" which it claims to be. Queen Victoria, who is visiting the show, under escort of Mr. Punch, remarks: "We have nothing of that sort, Mr. Punch; but should there be a *lion* show, we can send a specimen! !"

CHAPTER XV

THE STRUGGLE IN THE CRIMEA

THE grim struggle of the Crimean War for a time checked Mr. Punch's attacks upon Napoleon III., and turned his attention in another direction. Although the war cloud in the East was assuming portentous dimensions, there were many in England, the Peace Society, the members of the peace-at-any-price party, with Messrs. Bright and Cobden at their head, and most conspicuous of all the Prime Minister, Lord Aberdeen, who deliberately blinded themselves to the possibility of war. It was for the enlightenment of these gentlemen that Mr. Leech designed his cartoon " No Danger," representing a donkey, eloquent in his stolid stupidity, tranquilly braying in front of a loaded cannon. In still another cartoon Lord Aberdeen himself is placidly smoking " The Pipe of Peace " over a brimming barrel of gunpowder. John Bull, however, has already become wide-awake to the danger, for he is nailing the Russian eagle to his barn door, remarking to his French neighbor that *he* won't worry the Turkies any more. At this time England had begun to watch with growing jealousy the cordial *entente* between Russia and Austria, for the Emperor Nicholas was strongly suspected of having offered to Austria a slice of his prospective prize, Turkey. This rumor forms the basis of an effective cartoon by Leech, " The Old 'Un and the Young 'Un," in which the Russian and Austrian Emperors are seated at table, genially dividing a bottle of port between them. " Now then, Austria," says Nicholas, " just help me finish

the Port(e)."   Meanwhile, hostilities between Turkey and
Russia had begun, and the latter had already received a
serious setback at Oltenitza, an event commemorated by Tenniel in his cartoon of " A Bear with a Sore Head."   In spite
of his blind optimism, Lord Aberdeen was by this time finding
it decidedly difficult to handle the reins of foreign affairs.
One of the best satires of the year is by Tenniel, entitled
" The Unpopular Act of the Courier of St. Petersburg," depicting Aberdeen performing the dangerous feat of driving
a team of vicious horses.   The mettlesome leaders, Russia
and Turkey, have already taken the bit between their teeth,
while Austria, catching the contagion of their viciousness, is
plunging dangerously.   This cartoon was soon followed by
another still more notable, entitled " What It Has Come
To," one of those splendid animal pictures in which John
Tenniel especially excelled.   It shows us the Russian bear,
scampering off in the distance, while in the foreground Lord
Aberdeen is clinging desperately to the British lion, which has
started in mad pursuit, with his mane erect and his tail
stiffened like a ramrod; the lion plunges along, dragging
behind him the terrified premier, who is gasping out that he
can no longer hold him and is forced to " let him go."   At
the same time Mr. Leech also represented pictorially Lord
Aberdeen awakening to the necessity of war in his " Bombardment of Odessa."   The cartoon is in two parts,
representing respectively the English Premier and the Russian Emperor reading their morning paper.   " Bombardment
of Odessa," says Aberdeen.   " Dear me, this will be very
disagreeable to my imperial friend."   " Bombardment of
Odessa," says Nicholas; " confound it!   This will be very
annoying to dear old Aberdeen! "   In the following November the British victory of Inkerman, won against almost

hopeless odds, was witnessed by two members of the Russian imperial family. Leech promptly commemorated this fact in his picture of " The Russian Bear's Licked Cubs, Nicholas and Michael." The cartoon entitled the " Bursting of the Russian Bubble " appeared in *Punch,* October 14, 1854, just

BURSTING OF THE RUSSIAN BUBBLE.

after the battle of the Alma had taken place and part of the Russian fleet had been destroyed by the English and French ships at Sebastopol. This cartoon is by the hand of Leech. The Russian Emperor, Nicholas I., had boasted of the " irresistible power " which was to enable him to overthrow the allied forces gathered in the Crimea, and here the artist shows very graphically the shattering of this " irresistible power " and of the " unlimited means." Of all the cartoons which Leech produced there is none which enjoys a more enduring fame than the one entitled " General Février

Turned Traitor." Certainly no other in the whole series of Crimean War cartoons appearing in *Punch* compares with it in power. Yet splendid and effective as it is, there is in it a cruelty worthy of Grandville or Gillray, and when it appeared

"GENERAL FÉVRIER" TURNED TRAITOR.

"RUSSIA HAS TWO GENERALS IN WHOM SHE CAN CONFIDE—GENERALS JANVIER AND FEVRIER."—*Speech of the late Emperor of Russia.*

it caused a shudder to run through all England. The Russian Emperor had boasted in a speech on the subject of the Crimean War that, whatever forces France and England might be able to send to the front, Russia possessed two generals on whom she could always rely, General Janvier and

General Février. In other words, Nicholas I. cynically alluded to the hardship of the Russian winter, on which he counted to reduce greatly by death the armies of the Allies in the Crimea. But toward the end of the winter, the Emperor himself died of pulmonary apoplexy, after an attack of influenza. In a flash, Leech seized upon the idea. *General Février had turned traitor.* Under this title, the cartoon was published by *Punch* in its issue of March 10, 1855. General Février (Death in the uniform of a Russian general) is placing his deadly hand on the breast of Nicholas, and the icy cold of the Russian winter—the ally in whom the Emperor had placed his trust—has recoiled upon himself. The tragic dignity and grim significance of this cartoon made a deep impression upon Ruskin, who regarded it as representing in the art of caricature what Hood's " Song of the Shirt " represents in poetry. " The reception of the last-named woodcut," he says, " was in several respects a curious test of modern feeling. . . There are some points to be regretted in the execution of the design, but the thought was a grand one; the memory of the word spoken and of its answer could hardly in any more impressive way have been recorded for the people; and I believe that to all persons accustomed to the earnest forms of art it contained a profound and touching lesson. The notable thing was, however, that it offended persons *not* in earnest, and was loudly cried out against by the polite journalism of Society. This fate is, I believe, the almost inevitable one of thoroughly genuine work in these days, whether poetry or painting; but what added to the singularity in this case was that coarse heartlessness was even more offended than polite heartlessness."

As was but natural, the Anglo-French alliance against Russia is alluded to in more than one of Mr. Punch's Crimean

HENRI ROCHEFORT AND HIS LANTERN.

War cartoons.   One of the earliest is a drawing by Tenniel
of England and France typified by two fine specimens of
Guards of both nations standing back to back in friendly
rivalry of height, and Mr. Spielmann records in his " History
of Punch " that the cut proved so popular that under its title
of " The United Service : " it was reproduced broadcast on
many articles of current use and even served as a decoration
for the backs of playing cards.   Still another cartoon,
entitled " The Split Crow in the Crimea," represents England
and France as two huntsmen, hard on the track of a wounded
and fleeing two-headed bird !   " He's hit hard !—follow him
up ! " exclaimed the huntsmen.   In a French reproduction of
this cartoon, which is to be found in Armand Dayot's " Le
Second Empire," " Crow " is amusingly translated as *cou-
ronne* (crown), and the publishers of *Punch* are given as

BROTHERS IN ARMS.   THE FRENCH AND ENGLISH
TROOPS IN THE CRIMEA.

" MM. Breadburg, Agnew, et Cie." Another cartoon of the same period is called "Brothers in Arms." It shows a British soldier carrying on his back a wounded French soldier, and a French soldier carrying on his back a wounded Englishman. The two wounded men are clasping hands. There is no better evidence of the utter dearth of French caricature at this period than the fact that M. Dayot, whose indefatigable research has brought together a highly interesting collection of pictorial documents of all classes upon this period of French history, could find nothing in the way of a cartoon in his own country and was forced to borrow from *Punch* the few that he reproduces.

On the other side the Russian cartoonists were by no means backward in recording the events of the war and holding up the efforts of the Allies to pictorial derision. The Russian point of view has come down to us in a series of excellent prints published in St. Petersburg during the months of the conflict. In this warfare the Russians may be said to have borrowed from their enemies, for this series is essentially French in method and execution. All through this series England and France are shown buffeted about from pillar to post by the Conquering Bear. A description of one of these cartoons will give a fair general idea of the entire series. Sir Charles Napier, at a dinner given in his honor in London just before the departure of the Allied fleet for Kronstadt, has made the foolish boast that he would soon invite his hosts to dine with him in St. Petersburg. Of course the fleet never reached St. Petersburg, and the Russian artist satirically summed up the situation by depicting Sir Charles at the top of the mast, endeavoring by the aid of a large spy-glass to catch a sight of the Czar's capital.

Among the crude American lithographs of this period the

TURKEY, JOHN BULL & MONSIEUR FROG-EATER IN A BAD FIX.

AN AMERICAN CARTOON ON THE CRIMEAN WAR.

From the collection of the New York Historical Society.

Crimean War was not forgotten. A rather rare cartoon, entitled "Turkey, John Bull and M. Frog-Eater in a Bad Fix," is especially interesting as an evidence that American sympathy during the war was in a measure on the Russian side. The Russian General Menshikoff is standing on the heights of Sebastopol looking down smilingly and serenely on the discomfited allies, saying: "How do you do, gentlemen? Very happy to see you. You must be tired. Won't you walk in and take something?" John Bull, seriously wounded, is lying prostrate, bawling out: "Come, come, Turk, no dodging. Hulloa there! Is that the way you stick to your friends? The coat of my stomach is ruined, my wind nearly gone. I won't be able to blow for a month. Pull me out of this at any price! The devil take one party and his dam the other. I am getting sick of this business." By his side is the figure of a Frenchman just hit by a cannonball from one of the Russian guns, and crying out: "O! By damn! I not like such treat. I come tousand mile and spend ver much money to take someting from wid you, and you treat me as I vas van Villin! Scoundrel! Robbare!!"

In closing the subject of the Crimean War, it is worth while to call attention to one curious phase of the war as contained in the programme of a theatrical entertainment given by the French soldiers in the trenches of Sebastopol, December 23, 1855. The programme is headed "The Little Comic Review of the Crimea." It contains the announcement of the Tchernaia Theater, which four days later is to present three dramatic pieces. The drawing is by Lucien Salmont.

One final echo of the struggle in the Crimea is found in another of Tenniel's graphic animal pictures, "The British

PROGRAMME OF A THEATRICAL PERFORMANCE GIVEN BY THE FRENCH
SOLDIERS IN THE TRENCHES BEFORE SEBASTOPOL.

Lion Smells a Rat," which depicts an angry lion sniffing
suspiciously at the crack of a door, behind which is being held
the conference which followed the fall of Sebastopol.   But
by far the most famous instance of Tenniel's work is his
series of Cawnpore cartoons, the series bearing upon the
Indian mutiny of 1857; and one of the finest, if not the very
finest, of them all is that entitled " The British Lion's Vengeance on the Bengal Tiger."   It represents in the life work of
Tenniel what " General Février Turned Traitor " stands for
in the life work of John Leech.   The subject was suggested
to Tenniel by Shirley Brooks.   It summed up all the horror
and thirst for revenge which animated England when the
news came of the treacherous atrocities of the Sepoy rebels.
The Cawnpore massacre of women and children ordered by
the infamous Nána Sáhib had taken place in June, and when
this cartoon appeared in *Punch,* August 22, 1857, England
had just sent thirty thousand troops to India.   In the picture
the British lion is springing at the throat of the Bengal tiger,

THE BRITISH LION'S VENGEANCE ON THE BENGAL TIGER.

which is standing over the prostrate bodies of a woman and a child. The tiger, fearful of being robbed of its prey, is snarling at the avenging lion. Another of the famous Cawnpore cartoons of Tenniel is descriptive of British vengeance on the Sepoy mutineers. The English troops were simply wild for revenge when the stories came to them of the atrocities which had been perpetrated on English women and children, and their vengeance knew no bounds. The Sepoys were blown from the mouths of the English cannon. It was the custom of the English soldiers to pile up a heap of Sepoys, dead or wounded, pour oil over them, and then set fire to the pile. The Tenniel cartoon, entitled " Justice," published September 12, 1857, shows the figure of Justice with sword and shield cutting down the mutineers, while behind her are the British troops working destruction with their bayonets.

No sooner had the English-French alliance against Russia come to an end than *Punch* once more began to give expression to his disapproval of Napoleon. A hostile spirit toward Frenchmen was ingrained in the very nature of John Leech, and he vented it freely in such cartoons as his celebrated " Cock-a-doodle-doo! " in which the French cock, clad in the uniform of a colonel, is crowing lustily over the results of a war of which Great Britain had borne the brunt. Or again, in " Some Foreign Produce that Mr. Bull can very well Spare," a cut which includes French conspirators, vile Frenchwomen, organ-grinders (Mr. Leech was abnormally sensitive to street noises), and other objectionable foreign refuse. It is interesting in this connection to note that Leech's hostility to Louis Napoleon was the direct cause of Thackeray's resignation from the staff of *Punch* in the winter of 1854. In the letter written in the following March, Thackeray explains

that he had had some serious differences regarding the editorial policy of *Punch,* and more specifically about the abuse of
Louis Napoleon which, he says, " I think and thought was
writing unjustly at that time, and dangerously for the welfare
and peace of the country;" and he then adds the specific instance which prompted him to sever his connections: " Coming from Edinburgh, I bought a *Punch* containing a picture of
a beggar on horseback, in which the emperor was represented
galloping to hell with a sword reeking with blood. As soon
as ever I could, after my return, I went to Bouverie Street
and gave in my resignation." Thackeray's act had no influence upon the policy of *Punch.* Leech's cartoons grew steadily
more incisive in character. One of the most extraordinary is
that known as " The French Porcupine." It represents

THE FRENCH PORCUPINE.
He may be an Inoffensive Animal, but he Don't Look like it.

Napoleon III. as a porcupine, bristling with French bayonets
in place of quills. One of Napoleon's favorite sayings was
" *L'Empire c'est la paix."* But this saying was very often
contradicted by events, and the first ten years of his occupation of the French throne showed France embroiled in the
Crimean War and the war with Austria. In preparation for
the latter conflict a large increase was being made in the

French military armament; and Leech seized upon the emperor's dictum only to express his skepticism. The cartoon appeared in March, 1859. As a matter of fact, the idea in this cartoon had previously been used in another called " The Puppet Show," published in June, 1854, depicting the Czar Nicholas in a manner closely similar; yet Mr. Spielmann, who notes this fact, adds that Mr. Leech had probably never seen, or else had forgotten, the earlier caricature. This " French Porcupine " is cited as an instance of Leech's extraordinary speed in executing a cartoon directly upon the wooden block. The regular *Punch* dinner had that week been held a day late. " Every moment was precious, and Leech proposed the idea for the cartoon, drew it in two hours, and caught his midday train on the following day, speeding away into the country with John Tenniel for their usual Saturday hunt." It was during this same year, 1859, at the close of the war which humbled Austria and forced her to surrender Venetia to Sardinia, that Leech voiced the suspicion that Louis was casting longing eyes upon Italian territory in a cartoon entitled " A Scene from the New Pantomime." Napoleon III. here figures as a clown, a revolver in his hand, a goose labeled Italy protruding from his capacious pocket. He is earnestly assuring Britannia, represented as a stout, elderly woman, eying him suspiciously, that his intentions are strictly honorable.

PART III

THE CIVIL AND FRANCO-PRUSSIAN WARS

CHAPTER XVI

THE MEXICAN WAR AND SLAVERY

I N this country the political cartoon, which practically began with William Charles's parodies upon Gillray, developed in a fitful and spasmodic fashion until about the middle of the century. Their basis was the Gillray group of many figures, and they had also much of the Gillray coarseness and indecency, with a minimum of artistic skill. They were mostly lithographs of the crudest sort, designed to pass from hand to hand, or to be tacked up on the wall. It was not until the first administration of Andrew Jackson that a school of distinctly American political caricature can be said to have existed. It was in 1848 that the firm of Currier & Ives, with an office in Nassau Street, in New York City, began the publication of a series of campaign caricatures of sufficient merit to have been a serious factor in influencing public opinion. Crude as they are, these lithographs are exceedingly interesting to study in detail. They tell their story very plainly, even apart from the legends inclosed in the huge balloon-like loops issuing from the lips of each member of the group—loops that suggest a grotesque resemblance to a soap-bubble party on a large scale. There is an amusing stiffness about the figures. They stand in such painfully precise attitudes that at a little dis-

NEW EDITION OF MACBETH—BANK-OH'S GHOST! 1837.

One of the caricatures inspired by the United States Bank Case.

From the collection of the New York Public Library.

BALAAM AND BALAAM'S ASS.

One of the caricatures inspired by the United States Bank Case.

From the collection of the New York Public Library.

A NEW MAP OF THE UNITED STATES WITH THE ADDITIONAL TERRITORIES ON AN IMPROVED PLAN.
1828.

From the collection of the New York Public Library.

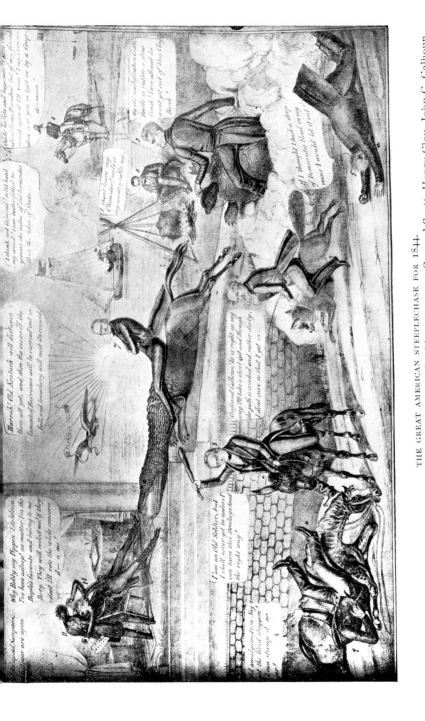

THE GREAT AMERICAN STEEPLECHASE FOR 1844.

Among the various candidates for the Presidency shown in this cartoon are General Scott, Henry Clay, John C. Calhoun, Daniel Webster, James Buchanan and Martin Van Buren.

From the collection of the New York Public Library.

tance they might readily be mistaken for some antiquated fashion plates. The faces, however, are in most cases excellent likenesses; they are neither distorted nor exaggerated. The artists, while sadly behind the times in retaining the use of the loop which Continental cartoonists discarded much earlier, were in other respects quite up-to-date, especially in adopting the method of the elder Doyle, whose great contribution to caricature was that of drawing absolutely faithful likenesses of the statesmen he wished to ridicule, relying for the humor of the cartoon upon the situation in which he placed them. It was only natural that the events of the Mexican War should have inspired a number of cartoons. One of these is entitled "Uncle Sam's Taylorifics," and shows a complacent Yankee coolly snipping a Mexican in two with a huge pair of shears. One blade bears the inscription "Volunteers," and the other "General Taylor." The Yankee's left arm is labeled "Eastern States," the tail of his coat "Oregon," his belt "Union," his left leg "Western States," and his right leg, which he is using vigorously on the Mexican, "Southern States," and the boot "Texas." Below the discomfited Mexican yawns the Rio Grande. Behind the Yankee's back John Bull—a John Bull of the type introduced by William Charles during the War of 1812—is looking on enviously.

American national feeling on the subject of the European Powers deriving benefit from the discovery of gold in California is illustrated by a cartoon which shows the United States ready to defend her possessions by force of arms. The various Powers have crossed the sea and are very near to our coast. Queen Victoria, mounted on a bull, is in the lead. She is saying: "Oh, dear Albert, don't you cry for me. I'm off for California with my shovel on my knee." Behind

UNCLE · SAM'S · TAYLORIFICS

THE **MEXICAN COMMANDER** ENJOYING THE PROSPECT OPPOSITE **MATAMORAS.**

Can I believe my spectacles? Bare these "Northern Barbarians" thus insult the "magnanimous Mexican Nation? They have taken Texas—They grasp at Oregon—Now they lay their "rapacious hand" on Mexico! "And is liberty!" where is my friend John Bull?

PUB. BY IW STRONG,98 NASSAU ST N.Y.

AMERICAN CARTOONS OF THE WAR WITH MEXICO.

From the collection of the New York Historical Society.

her is the figure of Russia, saying: " As something is Bruin, I'll put in my paw, while the nations around me are making a Jaw." Louis Napoleon, who at the time had just been elected President of the French, is drawn in the form of a bird. He is flying over the heads of Victoria and Russia, and singing: " As you have gold for all creation, den please give some to La Grand Nation. I have just become de President, and back I shall not like to went." In the distance may be seen Spain, and beyond the United States fleet. Along the shore stretch the tents of an American army. Ominously coiled up on the rocks is the American rattlesnake with the head of President Taylor. Back of the camp is a battery of American guns directed by the American eagle, which wears the head of General Scott, saying: " Retreat, you poor d——s! Nor a squabble engender, for our Gold unto you we will never surrender. Right about face! Double quick to the rear! And back to your keepers all hands of you steer."

The Presidential election of 1852 was cartooned under the title " Great Foot Race for the Presidential Purse ($100,-000 and Pickings) Over the Union Course, 1852." The Whigs, encouraged by their success with General Taylor, put forth another military officer, General Scott, as their candidate, but in this cartoon Daniel Webster is shown to be well in the lead and receiving the plaudits of most of the spectators. Behind him is Scott, and a little way back is Franklin Pierce, who proved the ultimate winner. " I can beat you both, and walk in at that, although you had a hundred yards the start of me," is Webster's conviction. " Confound Webster!" cries Scott. " What does he want to get right in my way for? If he don't give out, or Pierce don't faint, I shall be beaten." " No, no, old Fuss and Feathers," retorts

DEFENCE OF THE CALIFORNIA BANK

From the collection of the New York Historical Society.

GREAT FOOTRACE FOR THE PRESIDENTIAL PURSE ($100,000 AND PICKINGS) OVER THE UNION COURSE 1852.

From the collection of the New York Historical Society.

THE PRESIDENTIAL CAMPAIGN OF '56.

From the collection of the New York Historical Society.

"NO HIGHER LAW."

From the collection of the New York Historical Society.

Pierce, " you don't catch this child fainting now. I am going to make good time! Whether I win or not, Legs, do your duty."

Caricature dealing with the Presidential campaign of 1856 is represented by the cartoon called " The Presidential Campaign of '56." Buchanan, who proved the successful candidate, is mounted on a hideous monster resembling a snake, and marked " Slavery." The monster is being wheeled along on a low, flat car drawn by Pierce, Douglas, and Cass. A star bearing the word " Kansas " is about to disappear down the monster's throat. In the distance Fremont, on horseback, is calling out: " Hold on! Take that animal back! We don't want it this side of the fence." Buchanan is saying, " Pull down that fence and make way for the Peculiar Institution." The fence in question is the Mason and Dixon's line. The faces of Cass, Douglas, and Pierce, who are drawing along the monster, are obliterated— they are absolutely formless.

The evils of slavery from a Northern point of view are shown in a cartoon called " No Higher Law." King Slavery is seated on his throne holding aloft a lash and a chain. Under his left elbow is the Fugitive Slave Bill, resting on three human skulls. Daniel Webster stands beside the throne, holding in his hand the scroll on which is printed, " I propose to support that bill to the fullest extent—to the fullest extent." A runaway slave is fighting off the blood-hounds that are worrying him, and in the distance, on a hill, the figure of Liberty is toppling from her pedestal.

The cartoon " Practical Illustration of the Fugitive Slave Law " sums up very completely Abolitionist sentiment on the subject. The slaveholder, with a noose in one hand and a chain in the other, a cigar in his mouth and his top-hat

PRACTICAL ILLUSTRATION OF THE FUGITIVE SLAVE LAW.

From the collection of the New York Historical Society.

THE GREAT DISUNION SERPENT,

From the collection of the New York Historical Society.

decorated with the single star, which was the sign of the
Southern Confederacy, is astride of the back of Daniel Webster, who is crawling on all-fours.   In Webster's left hand
is the Constitution.   " Don't back out, Webster," says the
slaveholder.   " If you do, we're ruined."   The slave-woman
who is being pursued has taken refuge with William Lloyd
Garrison, of the Boston *Liberator,* who is saying: " Don't
be alarmed, Susanna, you're safe enough."   One of Garrison's arms is encircling the negress's waist, at the end of the
other is a pistol.   In the back of the picture is the Temple of
Liberty, over which two flags are flying.   On one flag we
read: " All men are born free and equal; " on the other,
" A day, an hour, of virtuous Liberty is worth an Age of
servitude."

CHAPTER XVII

DOWN to the last quarter of the nineteenth century, the history of American political caricature is a history of lost opportunities. Revolution and war have always been the great harvest times of the cartoonist. Gillray and Rowlandson owe their fame to the Napoleonic wars; Philipon and Daumier, to the overthrow of Louis Philippe; Leech and Tenniel reached their zenith in the days of the Crimean War and the Sepoy Mutiny. It is not the election cartoon, or the tariff cartoon, or the cartoon of local politics, it is the war cartoon that is most widely hailed and longest remembered. Yet of all the wars in which the United States has been engaged, not one has given birth to a great satiric genius, and none but the latest, our recent war with Spain, has received comprehensive treatment in the form of caricature. It is not strange that the Revolutionary War and that of 1812 failed to inspire any worthier efforts than William Charles's crude imitations of Gillray. The mechanical processes of printing and engraving, the methods of distribution, the standards of public taste, were all still too primitive. The Mexican War was commemorated in a number of the popular lithographs of the day; but it was not a prolonged struggle, nor one calculated to stir the public mind profoundly. With the Civil War the case was radically different. Here was a struggle which threatened not only national honor, but national existence—a struggle which prolonged itself grimly, month after month, and was borne home to a great majority of American families with the force of personal tragedy, arraying friend against friend, and father against son, and offering no brighter hope for the future than the vista of a steadily lengthening death-roll. There was never a time in the history of the nation when the public mind, from one end of the country to the other, was in such a state of tension; never, since the days of Napoleon, had there been such an opportunity for a real master of satiric art. It seems amazing, as one looks back

ROUGH AND READY LOCOMOTIVE AGAINST THE FIELD.

From the collection of the New York Historical Society.

over the pictorial records of these four years, that the magnitude of the events did not galvanize into activity some unknown genius of the pencil, and found then and there a new school of American caricature commensurate with the fever-heat of public sentiment. The existing school of caricature seems to have been absurdly inadequate. The prevailing

types were a sort of fashion-plate lithograph—groups of
public men in mildly humorous situations, their features fixed
in the solemn repose of the daguerreotypes upon which they
were probably modeled; or else the conventional election
steeplechase, in which the contestants, with long, balloon-like
loops trailing from their mouths, suggest an absurd semblance
to the cowboys of a Wild West show, all engaged in a vain
attempt to lasso and pull in their own idle words.   Many of
the cartoons actually issued at the outbreak of the Civil War
impress one with a sense of indecorum, of ill-timed levity.
What was wanted was not the ineptitude of feeble humor,
but the rancor and venom of a Gillray, the stinging irony of a
Daumier, the grim dignity of a Tenniel.   And it was not
forthcoming.   The one living American who might have
produced work of a high order was Thomas Nast; but
although Nast's pencil was dedicated to the cause of the
Union from the beginning to the end, in the series of powerful emblematic pictures that appeared in *Harper's Weekly,*
his work as a caricaturist did not begin until the close of the
war.

It is interesting to conjecture what the great masters of
caricature would have made of such an opportunity.   The
issues of the war were so clear-cut, their ethical significance so
momentous, that an American Gillray, a Unionist Gillray,
would have found material for a series of cartoons of
eloquent and grewsome power.   It is easy to imagine what
form they would have taken: an Uncle Sam, writhing in
agony, his limbs shackled with the chains of slavery, his lips
gagged with the Fugitive Slave Law, slowly being sawn
asunder, while Abolition and Secession guide the opposite
ends of the saw, or else the American Eagle being worried
and torn limb from limb by Southern bloodhounds and stung

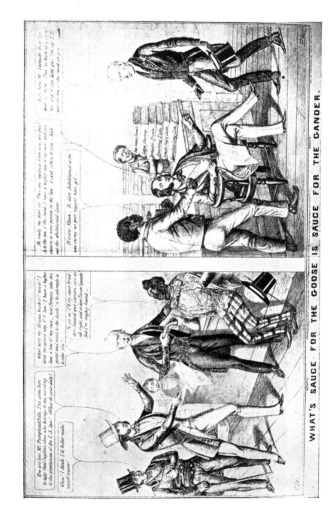

From the collection of the New York Historical Society.

by copperheads, while the British Lion and the rest of the
European menagerie look on, wistfully licking their chops
and with difficulty restraining themselves from participating
in the feast. Such a cartoonist would have found a mine of
suggestion in " Uncle Tom's Cabin "; he would have crowded
his plates with Legrees and Topsies, Uncle Toms and Sambos
and Quimbos, fearful and wonderful to look upon, brutal,
distorted, and unforgettable.

It is equally easy to imagine what a Daumier might have
done with the material afforded by the Civil War. Some
types of faces seem to defy the best efforts of the caricaturist
—smooth, regular-featured faces, like that of Lord Rosebery,
over which the pencil of satire seems to slip without leaving
any effective mark. Other faces, strong, rugged, salient,
seem to invite the caricaturist's efforts; and these were the
types that predominated among the leaders of the struggle
for the Union. Daumier's genius lay in his ability to caricature the human face, to seize upon a minimum of lines and
points, to catch some absurd semblance to an inanimate object,
some symbolic suggestion. And when once found, he would
harp upon it, ringing all possible changes, keeping it in-
sistently, mercilessly before the public. One can fancy with
what avidity he would have seized upon the stolid, indomit-
able figure of Grant, intrenched behind his big, black, ubiquitous cigar. That cigar would have become the center of
interest, the portentous symbol of Grant's dogged, taciturn
persistence. Gradually that cigar would have grown and
grown, its thickening smoke spreading in a dense war cloud
over the whole series of cartoons, until finally it became the
black, shining muzzle of a cannon, belching forth the powder
and fire and ammunition that was to decide the issue of the
war. What Tenniel would have done is evidenced by what

NAST'S FAMOUS CARTOON "PEACE."

he actually did in *Punch*. The great tragedies of those four years, Gettysburg and Bull Run and the Battle of the Wilderness, would have been pictured with the tragic dignity that stamps his famous cartoon in which he commemorated the assassination of Lincoln.

CHAPTER XVIII

THE SOUTH SECEDES

IN view of what might have been done, it is somewhat exasperating to look over the actual cartoons of the war as they have come down to us. Even when a clever idea was evolved none seemed to have the cleverness or the enterprise to develop it. As all the modern cartoonists realize, nothing is more effective than a well-planned series. It is like the constant dropping that wears away the stone. The most potent pictorial satire has always been the gradual elaboration of some clever idea—the periodic reappearance of the same characters in slightly modified environment, like the successive chapters of a serial story. The public learn to look forward to them, and hail each reappearance with a

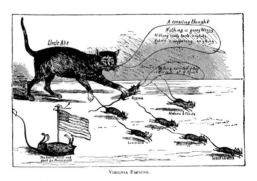

VIRGINIA PAUSING.

renewed burst of enthusiasm. The cartoonists of the Civil War do not seem to have grasped this idea. A single example will serve as an illustration. A clever cartoon, entitled " Virginia Pausing," appeared just at the time that Virginia, the last of the States to secede, joined the Con-

federacy.   The several Southern States, represented as young
rats, are gayly scampering off, in the order in which they
seceded, South Carolina heading the procession.   Virginia

SOME ENVELOPES OF THE TIME OF THE WAR.

straggling in the rear finds herself under the paw of " Uncle
Abe," represented as a watchful and alert old mouser, and
has paused, despite herself, to consider her next step.   The
Union, personified as the mother rat of the brood, lies stark
and stiff on her back, with the Stars and Stripes waving over
her corpse, and underneath, the legend, " The Union must
and shall be preserved."   Now this idea of the Southern
States as a brood of " Secession rats " was capable of infinite
elaboration.   It might have been carried on throughout the
entire four years of the struggle, the procession preserving the
same significant order, with South Carolina in the lead,

Virginia bringing up the rear, and Lincoln, as a wise and resourceful mouser, ever in-pursuit. It could have shown the rats at bay, cornered, entrapped—in short, the whole history of the war in a form of genial allegory. But if the initial cartoon, "Virginia Pausing," ever had a sequel, it perished in the general wreckage of the Confederacy.

The welcome which awaited caricature, even of the crudest sort, at the outbreak of the war is illustrated by the curious vogue enjoyed by envelopes adorned with all sorts of patriotic and symbolic devices—an isolated tombstone inscribed "Jeff Davis alone," a Confederate Mule, blanketed with the Stars and Bars—a slave-owner vainly brandishing his whip and shouting to a runaway slave, "Come back here, you black rascal." The latter, safe within the shadow of Fortress Monroe, defiantly places his thumb to his nose, and in allusion to General Butler's famous decision, retorts: "Can't come back, nohow, massa. Dis chile's CONTRABAN'."

It is not surprising to find that Lincoln throughout the struggle was a favorite subject for the caricaturist. His tall, ungainly, loose-knit figure, his homely features, full of noble resolve, seemed to offer a standing challenge to the cartoonist, who usually treated him with indulgent kindness. The exceptions are all the more con-

spicuous. A case in point is the cartoon commemorating
Lincoln's first call for volunteers for three months—a period
then supposed to be ample for crushing out the rebellion.
The artist has represented Lincoln as the image of imbecilic
dismay, while a Union soldier with a sternly questioning gaze

relentlessly presents to him a promissory note indorsed,
" I promise to subdue the South in 90 days. Abe Lincoln."
A much more typical and kindly cartoon of Lincoln is the one
representing him as emulating the feat of Blondin and cross-
ing the rapids of Niagara on a tight-rope, bearing the negro
problem on his shoulders, and sustaining his equipoise with
the aid of a balancing pole labeled " Constitution."

The really clever cartoons of this period are so few in
number, and stand out so prominently from a mass of second-
rate material, that there is real danger of attaching undue

importance to them.   Such a plate as " The Southern Confederacy a Fact!   Acknowledged by a Mighty Prince and
Faithful Ally," which was issued by a Philadelphia publisher
in 1861, although crudely drawn, is one of the very few that
show the influence of the early English school.   It represents
the Devil and his assembled Cabinet in solemn conclave, receiving the envoys of the Southern Confederacy.   The latter

includes, among others, Jeff Davis, General Beauregard, and
a personification of " Mr. Mob Law, Chief Justice."   They
are bearers of credentials setting forth the fundamental principles of the government, as " Treason, Rebellion, Murder,
Robbery, Incendiarism, Theft, etc."   Satan, interested in
spite of himself, is murmuring to his companions, " I am
afraid in Rascality they will beat us."

An effective allegorical cartoon, which appeared at a time

when the cause of the Union seemed almost hopeless, pictures
Justice on the rock of the Constitution dressed in the Stars
and Stripes and waving an American flag toward a happier
scene, where the sun of Universal Freedom is brightly shining.   Behind her are hideous scenes of disorder and national
disaster.   A loathsome serpent, of which the head is called
" Peace Compromise," the body, " Mason and Dixon's

Line," and the tail " Copperhead," is crawling up the rock
seeking to destroy her.   In one of its coils it is crushing out
the lives of a number of black women and children.   In one
corner of the cartoon the figure of a winged Satan is hovering
gleefully over a mob which is hanging a negro to a lamp-
post—an allusion to the Draft Riots in New York.   Some of
the mob are bearing banners with the words " Black Men
have no Rights."   In the shadowy background of the picture

a slaveholder is lashing his slave, tied to a post, with a whip
called "Lawful Stimulant."   An unctuous capitalist is talking with a group of Secessionists, seated on a rock called
"State Rights."   In contrast with the dark picture on which
Justice has turned her back is the bright vista of the future,
"The Union as it will be," into which she is looking.   There
we see a broad river and a prosperous city.   A negress, free
and happy, is sewing by her cabin door, her child reading a
book upon her knee.

M^r MOB LAW   G^{en'l} BEAUREGARD   S^{ec} TOOMBS   JEFF DAVIS   Vice Pres STEPHENS   THE PRINCE TO HIS CABINET
Chief Justice   *I am relieved my Honest Lords they will treat us*

THE SOUTHERN CONFEDERACY A FACT !!!

ACKNOWLEDGED BY A MIGHTY PRINCE AND FAITHFUL ALLY

Lithogh Publd. 600 Chestnut St. Philad^a J^{no} Story

From the collection of the New York Historical Society.

From the collection of the New York Historical Society.

CHAPTER XIX

THE FOUR-YEARS' STRUGGLE

MANY of the best cartoons of the period revolve around the rivalry between General McClellan and General Grant, and the incidents of the McClellan-Lincoln campaign of 1864. "The Old Bull-dog on the Right Track" is one of the best products of the war cartoonists. It represents Grant as a thoroughbred bull-dog, seated in dogged tenacity of purpose on the "Weldon Railroad," and preparing to fight it out on that line, if it takes all summer. At the end of the line is a kennel, labeled "Richmond," and occupied by a pack of lean, cowardly hounds, Lee, Davis, and Beauregard among the number, who are yelping: "You aint got the kennel yet, old fellow!" A bellicose little dwarf, McClellan, is advising the bulldog's master: "Uncle Abraham, don't you think you had better

call the old dog off now? I'm afraid he'll hurt these other dogs, if he catches hold of them!" To which President Lincoln serenely rejoins: "Why, little Mac, that's the same pack of curs that chased you aboard of the gunboat two years

175

From the collection of the New York Historical Society.

ago. They are pretty nearly used up now, and I think it's best to go in and finish them."

The conservative policy which marked the military career of General McClellan and his candidacy for the Presidency in 1864 is ridiculed in a cartoon entitled " Little Mac, in His Great Two-Horse Act, in the Presidential Canvass of 1864." Here McClellan is pictured as a circus rider about to come to grief, owing to the unwillingness of his two steeds to pull together in harmony. A fiery and stalwart horse represents " war "; while peace is depicted as a worthless and broken-down hack. Little Mac is saying, " Curse them balky horses—I can't manage the Act nohow. One threw me in Virginia, and the other is bound the wrong way." In the background is the figure of Lincoln attired as a clown. " You tried to ride them two horses on the Peninsula for two years, Mac," he calls out, " but it wouldn't work."

Another striking cartoon of this Presidential campaign depicts the Republican leaders burying the War Democracy. The cartoon is called " The Grave of the Union," and was drawn by Zeke. The hearse is being driven by Secretary Stanton, who commenced, " My jackasses had a load, but they pulled it through bravely." In harness and attached to the bodies of jackasses are the heads of Cochrane, Butler, Meagher, and Dickinson. At the head of the grave, a sort of master of ceremonies, is the familiar figure of Horace Greeley, saying, " I guess we'll bury it so deep that it will never get up again." By his side is Lincoln, who is inquiring, " Chase, will it stay down? " to which Chase replies, " My God, it must stay down, or we shall go up." The funeral service is being conducted by Henry Ward Beecher, who is carrying a little negro in his arms. " Not thy will, O Lord, but mine be done." Beecher is reading from the book before

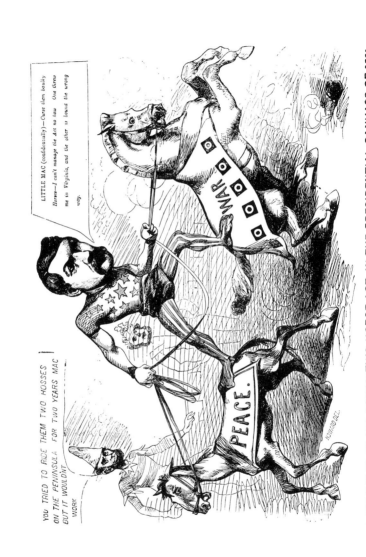

LITTLE MAC, IN HIS GREAT TWO HORSE ACT, IN THE PRESIDENTIAL CANVASS OF 1864.

From the collection of the New York Historical Society.

him. The coffins about to be lowered into the grave are
marked respectively " Free Speech and Free Press," " Ha-
beas Corpus," and " Union."

One of the most striking caricatures suggested by the contest between Lincoln and McClellan for the Presidency of
1864 is entitled " The Abolition Catastrophe; or, the November Smash-up." It is really nothing more than the old
hackneyed idea of the " Presidential Steeplechase " presented
in a new guise. The artist, however, proved himself to be a
false prophet. It shows a race to the White House between
two trains, in which the one on which Lincoln is serving as
engineer has just come to destruction on the rocks of " Eman-
cipation," " Confiscation," and " $400,000,000,000 Public
Debt." The train in the charge of General McClellan, its
locomotive flying the flag " Constitution," is running along
smoothly and rapidly and is just turning the curve leading up
to the door of the White House. McClellan, watching from
his cab the discomfiture of his foe, calls derisively, " Wouldn't
you like to swap horses now, Lincoln? " In the coaches
behind are the elated passengers of the Democratic train.
In striking contrast is the plight in which the Republican
Party is shown. Lincoln, thrown up in the air by the shock
of the collision, calls back to his rival, " Don't mention it,
Mac, this reminds me of a "—an allusion to the President's
fondness for illustrating every argument with a story. From
the debris of the wreck of the locomotive peer out the faces
of the firemen—two very black negroes. One is calling,
" War's de rest ob dis ole darky? Dis wot yer call 'manci-
pation? " And the other, " Lor' A'mighty! Massa Lin-
cum, is dis wot yer call Elewating de Nigger? " The passengers behind are in an equally unhappy strait. Secretary
Stanton, pinned under the wheels of the first coach, is crying,

" Oh, dear! If I could telegraph this to Dix I'd make it out
a victory." Among the passengers may be recognized the
countenances of Beecher, Butler, and Seward, while blown up

From the collection of the New York Historical Society.

in the air is Horace Greeley, calling out to Lincoln that the
disaster only verifies the prediction which had been printed
in the *Tribune*. Popular discontent at the unreliability of
news of the war found utterance in a skit representing Lincoln
as a bartender occupied in concocting a mixed drink, called
" New York Press," which he is dexterously pouring back and
forth between two tumblers, labeled respectively " Victory "
and " Defeat." The ingredients are taken from bottles of
" Bunkum," " Bosh," " Brag," and " Soft Sawder."

From the collection of the New York Historical Society.

THE BLOCKADE ON THE "CONNECTICUT PLAN".

Respectfully dedicated to the Secretary of the Navy.

From the collection of the New York Historical Society.

In the same series as the " Abolition Catastrophe " is a cartoon entitled " Miscegenation; or, the Millennium of Abolition," intended to depict the possible alarming consequences of proclaiming the whole colored race free and equal. It humorously depicts a scene in which there is absolute social equality between the whites and the blacks. At one end of the picture Mr. Lincoln is receiving with great warmth and cordiality Miss Dinah Arabella Aramintha Squash, a negress of unprepossessing appearance, who has as her escort Henry Ward Beecher. At a table nearby Horace Greeley is treating another gorgeously attired negress to ice cream. Two repulsive-looking negroes are making violent love to two white women. A passing carriage in charge of a white coachman and two white footmen contains a negro family. In the back-

From the collection of the New York Historical Society.

ground, Englishmen, Frenchmen, and others are expressing their astonishment at the condition in which they find American society.

The attempt at escape, the apprehension and the incarceration of the President of the Confederacy are illustrated in a long series of cartoons. Two of the best are "The Confederacy in Petticoats" and "Uncle Sam's Menagerie."

THE CONFEDERACY IN PETTICOATS.

From the collection of the New York Historical Society.

The first deals with the capture of Jefferson Davis at Irwinsville by General Wilson's cavalry. Davis, attired in feminine dress, is climbing over a fence in order to escape his pursuers. He has dropped his handbag, but he still holds his unsheathed knife. "I thought your government was too magnanimous to hunt down women and children," he calls out to the Union soldiers, one of whom has caught him by the skirts and is trying to drag him back. Mrs. Davis, by her husband's side, is entreating, " Don't irritate the President. He might hurt somebody."

The cartoon " Uncle Sam's Menagerie " shows Davis in captivity at Fortress Monroe. The Confederate president is depicted as a hyena in a cage, playing with a human skull. An Uncle Sam of the smooth-faced type in which he at first appeared is the showman. Round Davis's neck is a noose

From the collection of the New York Historical Society.

connecting with a huge gallows and the rope is about to be drawn taut, while from an organ below the cage a musician is grinding out the strain, " Yankee Doodle." In the shape of birds perched on little gallows of their own above the President's cage, each with a noose around his neck, are the figures of the other leaders of the Confederacy. A crow is pecking at a grinning skull under which is written " Booth."

To this skull Uncle Sam is playfully pointing with his show-man's cane.

Alleged Republican intimidation at the poles in the election of 1864 is assailed in a cartoon representing a Union soldier about to cast his vote for McClellan. A thick-lipped negro stands guard over the ballot box, rifle in hand. He presents the point of the bayonet at the soldier's decorated breast. "Hallo, dar!" he calls out threateningly, "you can't put in

HOW FREE BALLOT IS PROTECTED!

From the collection of the New York Historical Society.

dat, you copper-head traitor, nor any odder, 'cept for Massa Lincoln." To which the soldier sadly replies, "I am an American citizen and did not think I had fought and bled for this. Alas, my country!" A corrupt election clerk is regarding the scene with disquiet. "I'm afraid we shall have trouble if that soldier is not allowed to vote," he says.

To which a companion cynically replies, " Gammon him, just turn round; you must pretend you see nothing of the kind going on, and keep on counting your votes."

THE NATION MOURNING AT LINCOLN'S BIER.
By Tenniel in " Punch."

CHAPTER XX

IN looking over the historical and political caricature of the nineteenth century, one very naturally finds several different methods of treatment and subdivision suggesting themselves. First, there is the obvious method of chronological order, which is being followed in the present volume, and which commended itself as being at once the simplest and the most comprehensive. It is the one method by which the history of the century may be regarded as the annals of a family of nations—a grotesque family of ill-assorted quadrupeds and still more curious bipeds, stepping forth two by two from the pages of comic art as from the threshold of some modern Noah's ark—Britannia and the British lion, Columbia and Uncle Sam, India and the Bengal tiger, French Liberty and the imperial eagle. It is the one method which focuses the attention upon the inter-relation, the significant groupings of these symbolic figures, and disregards their individual and isolated actions. What the Russian bear, the British lion, are doing in the seclusion of their respective fastnesses is of vastly less interest than the spectacle of the entire royal menagerie of Europe uniting in an effort to hold Napoleon at bay. In other words, this method enables us to pass lightly over questions of purely national interest and home policy—the Corn Laws of England, the tariff issues in the United States—and to keep the eye centered upon the really big dramas of history, played upon an international stage. It subordinates caricature itself to

the sequence of great events and great personages. It is the
Emperor Napoleon, his reign and his wars, and not the
English caricaturist Gillray; it is Louis Philippe, the bourgeois king, and not Philipon and Daumier, who form the
center of interest. In other words, from the present point
of view, the caricature itself is not so much the object looked
at as it is a powerful and clairvoyant lens through which we
may behold past history in the curiously distorted form in
which it was mirrored back by contemporary public opinion.

Other methods, however, might be used effectively, each
offering some special advantage of its own. For instance,
the whole history of the nineteenth century might be divided,

FIGURES FROM A TRIUMPH.

so to speak, geographically. The separate history of each nation might have been followed down in turn—the changing fortunes of England, typified by John Bull; of Russia in the guise of the bear; of the United States under the forms of the swarthy, smooth-faced Jonathan of early days, and the pleasanter Uncle Sam of recent years; and of France, typified at different times as an eagle, as a Gallic cock, as an angry goddess, and as a plump, pleasant-faced woman in a tricolored petticoat. Again, if it were desirable to emphasize

THE DIAGNOSIS.

" A bad régime during ten years   All your trouble comes from that. You will soon become convalescent with a good constitution and fewer leeches."

the development of comic art rather than its influence in history, one might group the separate divisions of the subject around certain schools of caricature, dealing first with Gillray, Rowlandson, and their fellows among the allied Continental nations; passing thence to the caricaturists of 1830, and thence carrying the sequence through Leech, Cham,

THE EGEREAN NYMPH.
By Daumier.

Tenniel, Nast, down to the caricaturists who in the closing years of the century developed the scope of caricature to a hitherto unparalleled extent. Still again, the history of the century in caricature might be traced along from some peculiarity, greatly exaggerated, of some great man to another personal peculiarity of some other great man; leaping from the tri-cornered hat of the Emperor Napoleon to the great nose of the Iron Duke, then on to the toupet and pear-shaped countenance of Louis Philippe, the emaciation of Abraham Lincoln, the grandpa's hat of the Harrison administration, the forehead curl of Disraeli, the collar of Gladstone, the turned-up moustaches of the Emperor William, and the prominent teeth of Mr. Roosevelt. This feature of the caricature seems important enough to justify a brief digression. It forms one of the foundation stones of the art, second only in importance to the conventionalized symbols of the different nations. From the latter the cartoonist builds up the century's history as recorded in its great events. From the former he traces that history as recorded in the personality of its great men.

The cartoons in which these different peculiarities of per-

PAUL AND VIRGINIA.
By Gill.

sonal appearance are emphasized cover the whole range of caricature, and the whole gamut of public opinion which inspired it. Here we may find every degree of malice, from

the fierce goggle eyes and diabolical expression which Gillray introduced into his portraits of the hated Bonaparte down
to the harmless exaggeration of the collar points by which
Furniss good-naturedly satirized the appearance of Mr.
Gladstone. Again, in this respect caricature varies much,
because all the great men of the century did not offer to the
caricaturists the same opportunities in the matter of unusual
features or personal eccentricities.

The authentic portraits and contemporary descriptions of
the first Napoleon show us that he was a man whose appearance was marred by no particular eccentricity of feature, and

THE FIRST CONSCRIPT OF FRANCE.
By Gill.

that the cartoons of which he is the principal subject are
largely allegorical, or inspired by the artist's intensity of
hatred. One German caricaturist, by a subtle distortion and
a lengthening of the cheeks and chin, introduced a resem-

blance to a rapacious wolf while preserving something of the real likeness. But in the goggle-eyed monsters of Gillray there is nothing save the hat and the uniform which suggests the real Napoleon. It was a sort of incarnation of Beelzebub which Gillray wished to draw and did draw, a monstrosity designed to rouse the superstitious hatred of the ignorant and lower classes of England, and to excite the nation to a warlike frenzy. The caricature aimed at Bonaparte's great rival, the conqueror of Waterloo, was produced in more peaceful times, was the work of his own countryman, was based mainly on party differences, and, naturally enough, it was in the main good-natured and kindly. Wellington in caricature may be summed up by saying that it was all simply an exaggeration of the size of his nose. The *poire* drawn into resemblance of the countenance of Louis Philippe was originally innocent enough, and had it been entirely ignored by the monarch and his ministers, would probably have had no political effect, and in the course of a few years been entirely forgotten. But being taken seriously and characterized as seditious, it acquired an exaggerated significance which may almost be said to have led to the revolution of 1848 and the establishment of the Second Republic. From the rich material offered by our War of Secession the caricaturists drew little more than the long, gaunt figure and the scraggy beard of Lincoln, and the cigar of General Grant. The possibilities of this cigar, as they probably would have been brought out by an artist like Daumier, have been suggested in an earlier chapter. It was the goatee of Louis Napoleon that was exaggerated to give a point to most of the cartoons in which he was a figure, although during the days of his power there were countless caricatures which drew suggestions from the misadventures of his early life,

his alleged experiences as a waiter in New York and a policeman in London, his escape from prison in the clothes of the
workman Badinguet (a name which his political enemies ap-

THE SITUATION.
By Gill.

plied to him very freely), and the fiasco at Strasburg. No
men of their time were more freely caricatured than Disraeli
in England and Thiers in France, for no men offered more to
the caricaturist, Disraeli being at once a Jew and the most
exquisite of affected dandies, and Thiers being, with the exception of Louis Blanc, the smallest man of note in France.
In one cartoon in *Punch*, Disraeli was figured as presiding
over " Fagin's Political School." In another he was represented as a hideous Oriental peri fluttering about the gates
of Paradise. Thiers's large head and diminutive stature
are subjects of countless cartoons, in which he is shown
emerging from a wineglass or concealed in a waistcoat

pocket, although *Punch* once humorously depicted him as Gulliver bound down by the Lilliputians.

If one were to attempt to draw a broad general distinction between French and English caricature throughout the century, it would be along the line of English superiority in the matter of satirizing great events, French superiority in satirizing great men.   The English cartoonists triumphed in the art of crowded canvases and effective groupings; the French in seizing upon the salient feature of face or form, and by a grotesque distortion, a malicious quirk, fixing upon their luckless subject a brand of ridicule that refused to be forgotten.   Although the fashion of embodying fairly recognizable portraits of prominent statesmen in caricatures became general in England early in the century, for a long time the effect was marred by their lack of facial expression. From situations of all sorts, ranging from high comedy to deadly peril and poignant suffering, the familiar features of British statesmen look forth placid, unconcerned, with the fixed, impersonal stare of puppets in a Punch-and-Judy show.   No French artist ever threw away his opportunities in such a foolish, spendthrift manner.   Even where the smooth, regular features of some especially characterless face gave little or nothing for a satiric pencil to seize upon, a Daumier or a Gill would manufacture a ludicrous effect through the familiar device of a giant's head on a dwarf's body, or the absurdly distorted reflection of a cylindrical mirror.   But by the time hostilities broke out between France and Prussia facial caricature had become an important factor in the British school of satire, as exemplified in the weekly pages of *Punch*.

CHAPTER XXI

THE OUTBREAK OF THE FRANCO-PRUSSIAN WAR

THIS was very natural, because the history of these years was largely a history of individuals. During the years between the close of the Civil War and the outbreak of war between France and Prussia the three dominant figures in European political caricature were the French Emperor, Prince Bismarck, and Benjamin Dis-

LOUIS BLANC.

raeli. Since 1848, Louis Napoleon had been the most widely caricatured man in Europe; and the outcome of the War of 1866 had raised Bismarck, as the pilot of the Prussian ship

of state, to an importance second only to Napoleon himself.
The caricature of which Disraeli was the subject was necessarily much narrower in its scope, and confined to a great
extent to England. It was not until the century's eighth

RIVAL ARBITERS.
Napoleon and Bismarck at the time of the
Austro-Prussian War.
By Tenniel in Punch.

decade that he received full recognition at the hands of the
Continental caricaturists, and his prominence in the cartoons
preceding the Franco-Prussian War was due to the prestige
of *Punch*, and to the opportunity which his own peculiar
personality and striking appearance offered to the caricaturists. It was not long after the fall of Richmond and the
end of the war that the agitation over the claims of the
United States against England on account of the damage
done by the warship *Alabama*, a question which was not

settled until a number of years later, began. The two powers
for a time could not agree on any scheme of arbitration, and
the condition of affairs in the autumn of 1865 was summed
up by Tenniel in *Punch,* in a cartoon entitled " The Disputed
Account," in which the United States and England are represented as two haggling women and Madame Britannia is
haughtily saying: " Claim for damages against me? Nonsense, Columbia! Don't be mean over money matters."
But England, as well as America, had other matters besides
the *Alabama* claims to disturb her and to keep busy the

THE MAN WHO LAUGHS.
By André Gill.

pencils of her cartoonists. Besides purely political issues at
home, there were the Jamaica troubles and Fenianism; and
the French Emperor was very urgent that stronger extradition treaties should be established between the two countries.

This last issue was cleverly hit off by *Punch* in a cartoon
which pictures Britannia showing Napoleon the Third a
portrait of himself as he appeared in 1848 and saying:
" That, Sire, is the portrait of a gentleman whom I should
have had to give up to the French Government had I always
translated 'extradition' as your Majesty's lawyers now

THE MAN WHO THINKS.
By André Gill.

wish." The agitation over the Jamaica troubles died out,
the threatened Fenian invasion of Canada came to nothing,
Louis Napoleon withdrew the French troops from Mexico,
and the eyes of Europe were directed toward the war cloud
hovering over Prussia and Austria. Early in June, 1866,
there was a cessation of diplomatic relations between the

two countries, followed immediately by a declaration of war on the part of Prussia, whose armies straightway entered Saxony and Hanover. The attitude of England and France toward the belligerents was the subject of *Punch's* cartoon that week. It was called " Honesty and Policy," and shows Britannia and Napoleon discussing the situation, while in the background the Prussian King and the Austrian Emperor are shaking their fists in each other's faces. Britannia con-

" TO BE OR NOT TO BE."
By Gill.

fides regretfully to Napoleon: " Well, I've done my best. If they must smash each other, they must." And the French Emperor says in a gleeful aside: " And someone may pick up the pieces! " The same figure of speech is further developed in a later cartoon which appeared in August, during the negotiations for peace. Napoleon III., in the guise of a ragpicker, is being warned off the Königstrasse by Bis-

marck: " Pardon, mon ami, but we really can't allow you
to pick up anything here; " and " Nap. the Chiffonnier "
rejoins: " Pray, don't mention it, M'sieu! It's not of the
slightest consequence."

After the battle of Sadowa, Austria accepted readily the
offer of the French Emperor to bring about a suspension of
hostilities, the Emperor of Austria agreeing to cede Venetia,
which was handed over to France, as a preliminary to its
cession to Italy. Tenniel pictured this event in a cartoon

ACHILLES IN RETREAT.
By Gill.

showing Napoleon acting as the temporary keeper of the
Lion of St. Mark's. Bismarck was now becoming a conspicuous figure in European politics, and his rivalry to Napoleon
is shown in a *Punch* cartoon entitled " Rival Arbiters," which
appeared about this time.

The growing spirit of discontent in France during the year or two immediately preceding the Franco-Prussian War was made the subject of some excellent *Punch* cartoons. One of these, called " Easing the Curb," appeared in July, 1869. The imperial rule was gradually becoming unpopular, and the opposition gaining in strength and boldness. The Em-

THE PRESIDENT OF RHODES.
By Daumier.

peror found it prudent to announce that it was his intention to grant to the French Chamber a considerable extension of power. In " Easing the Curb," *Punch* depicts France as a horse drawing the imperial carriage. Within are the Empress and the Prince Imperial, evidently greatly alarmed.

Napoleon is standing at the horse's head, calling out: "Have no fear, my dears. I shall just drop ze curb a leetel." In another cartoon a few months later, Napoleon the Third is shown wearing the crown of King John, and surrounded by

A TEMPEST IN A GLASS OF WATER.
By Gill.

a group of persistent barons, signing a magna charta for France.

In the pages of *Punch* from July, 1870, until the spring of 1871, one may follow very closely the history of the Franco-Prussian War and of the Commune. The first of the cartoons on this subject, published just before the declaration of war, is entitled "A Duel to the Death." In it the King of Prussia and the French Emperor are shown as duellists, sword in hand, while Britannia is endeavoring to act as mediator. "Pray stand back, madam," says Napoleon. "You

mean well, but this is an old family quarrel and we must fight
it out." *Punch* seemed to have an early premonition of
what the result of the war would be, for, before any decisive
battle had been fought, it published a striking cartoon entitled " A Vision on the Way," representing the shade of the
great Napoleon confronting the Emperor and his son on the
warpath, and bidding them " Beware ! "   The departure of

A DUEL TO THE DEATH.
By Tenniel in " Punch."

the Prince Imperial to the front is made the subject of a very
pretty and pathetic cartoon called " Two Mothers."   It shows
the Empress bidding farewell to her son, while France, as
another weeping mother, is saying: " Ah, madam, a sure
happiness for *you*, sooner or later; but there were dear sons of
mine whom I shall never see again."

CHAPTER XXII

THE DÉBÀCLE

AFTER the unimportant engagement at Saarbrück disaster began falling thick and fast on the French arms, and soon we find *Punch* taking up again the idea of the two monarchs as rival duelists. By this time the duel has been decided. Louis Napoleon, sorely wounded and

FRANCE, SEPTEMBER 4, 1870.
" Aux armes, citoyens,
Formez vos bataillons."

with broken sword, is leaning against a tree. " You have fought gallantly, sir," says the King. " May I not hear you say you have had enough? " To which the Emperor replies:

" I have been deceived about my strength. I have no choice."
With Sedan, the downfall of the Empire, and the establishment of the Republic, France ceased to be typified under the
form of Louis Napoleon. Henceforth she became an angry,
blazing-eyed woman, calling upon her sons to rise and repel
the advance of the invader. The cartoon in *Punch* commemorating September 4, 1870, when the Emperor was formally
deposed and a Provisional Government of National Defense
established under the Presidency of General Trochu, with

HER BAPTISM OF FIRE.
By Tenniel in " Punch."

Gambetta, Favre, and Jules Ferry among its leading members, shows her standing erect by the side of a cannon, the
imperial insignia trampled beneath her feet, waving aloft the
flag of the Republic, and shouting from the " Marseillaise " :

" Aux armes, citoyens,
Formez vos bataillons! "

The announcement that the German royal headquarters was to be removed to Versailles, and that the palace of Louis XIV. was to shelter the Prussian King surrounded by his conquering armies, drew from Tenniel the cartoon in which he showed the German monarch seated at his table in the palace studying the map of Paris, while in the background are the ghosts of Louis XIV. and the great Napoleon. The

ANDRÉ GILL.

ghost of the Grand Monarque is asking sadly: " Is this the end of ' all the glories '? " The sufferings of Paris during the siege are summed up in a cartoon entitled " Germany's Ally," in which the figure of Famine is laying its cold, gaunt hand on the head of the unhappy woman typifying the stricken city. The beginning of the bombardment was commemorated in a cartoon entitled " Her Baptism of Fire," showing the grim and bloody results of the falling of the

LE MARQUIS AUX TALONS ROUGES.

By Willette.

The Marquis de Galliffet will be remembered
as the French Minister of War during the second Dreyfus trial.   It was Willette's famous
cartoon of Queen Victoria which stirred up so
much ill feeling during the Boer War.

first shells. The whole tone of *Punch* after the downfall of
the Emperor shows a growing sympathy on the part of the
English people toward France, and the feeling in England
that Germany, guided by the iron hand of Bismarck, was
exacting a cruel and unjust penalty entirely out of proportion.
This belief that the terms demanded by the Germans were
harsh and excessive is shown in the *Punch* cartoon " Excessive
Bail," where Justice, after listening to Bismarck's argument,

says that she cannot "sanction a demand for exorbitant securities."

French caricature during " the terrible year " which saw Gravelotte, Sedan, and the downfall of the Empire was necessarily somber and utterly lacking in French gayety. It was not until the tragic days of the Siege and the Commune that the former strict censorship of the French press was

THE HISTORY OF A REIGN.
By Daumier in " Charivari."

"THIS HAS KILLED THAT."

By Daumier in " Charivari."

THE MOUSE-TRAP AND ITS VICTIMS.
By Daumier in " Charivari."

relaxed, and the floodgates were suddenly opened for a veritable inundation of cartoons.   M. Armand Dayot, in his
admirable pictorial history of this epoch, which has already
been frequently cited in the present volume, says in this connection: " It has been said with infinite justice that when art

is absent from caricature nothing remains but vulgarity." In proof of this, one needs only to glance through the albums containing the countless cartoons that appeared during the Siege, and more especially during the Commune. Aside from those signed by Daumier, Cham, André Gill, and a few other less famous artists, they are unclean compositions, without

PRUSSIA ANNEXES ALSACE.
By Cham in " Charivari."

design or wit, odious in color, the gross stupidity of their legends rivaling their lamentable poverty of execution. But under the leadership of Daumier, the small group of artists who infused their genius into the weekly pages of *Charivari,* made these tragic months one of the famous periods in the annals of French caricature. Of the earlier generation, the irrepressible group whose mordant irony had hastened the downfall of Louis Philippe, Daumier alone survived to chronicle by his pencil the disasters which befell France, with a talent as great as he had possessed thirty-odd years before, when engaged in his light-hearted and malicious campaign against the august person of Louis Philippe.   Then there

" Oh, no !   Prussia has not completely slain her.   It is not yet time to go to her aid."
By Cham in "Charivari."

were the illustrious " Cham " (Comte de Noë), and André Gill (a caricaturist of striking wit), Hadol, De Bertall, De Pilopel, Faustin, Draner, and a number of others not so well known.   But, above all, it was Daumier who, after twenty years of the Empire, during which his pencil had been politically idle, returned in his old age to the fray with all the vigor of the best days of *La Caricature.*

Yet to those whose sympathies were with France during the struggle of 1870-71, there is a distinct pathos in the change that is seen in the later work of Daumier—not a personal pathos, but a pathos due to the changed condition of the country which it reflects. The old dauntless audacity, the trenchant sarcasm, the mocking, light-hearted laughter, is gone. In its place is the haunting bitterness of an old man, under the burden of an impotent wrath—a man who, for all that he dips his pencil in pure vitriol, cannot do justice to the nightmare visions that beset him. There is no better commentary upon the pervading feeling of helpless anger and outraged national pride of this epoch than in these haunting designs of Daumier's. They are the work of a man tremulous with feverish indignation, weird and ghastly conceptions, such as might have emanated from the caldron of Macbeth's

" Adieu ! "
" No, ' au revoir.' Visits must be returned."
By Cham.

witches. The backgrounds are filled in with solid black, like a funeral pall; and from out the darkness the features of Bismarck, of Von Moltke, of William I., leer malevolently, distorted into hideous, ghoulish figures—vampires feasting upon the ruin they have wrought. French liberty, in the guise of a wan, emaciated, despairing figure, the personification of a wronged and outraged womanhood, haunts Daumier's pages. At one time she is standing, bound and gagged, between the gaping muzzles of two cannon marked, respectively, " Paris, 1851," and " Sedan, 1870," and underneath the laconic legend, " Histoire d'un Régne."

Another cartoon shows France as a female Prometheus bound to the rock, her vitals being torn by the Germanic vul-

SOUVENIRS AND REGRETS.
By Aranda.

ture. A number of these cartoons, all of which appeared in *La Charivari,* treat bitterly of the disastrous results of the twenty years during which Louis Napoleon was the Emperor of the French. The sketch called " This Has Killed That " has allusion to the popular ballot which elected the Prince-President to the throne. A gaunt, angry female figure is

THE SHOW OF THE NAPOLEONIC MOUNTEBANKS.

From a caricature by Hadol.

PRUSSIA INTRODUCING THE NEW NATIONAL ASSEMBLY TO FRANCE.

By Daumier in " Charivari."

pointing with one hand to the ballot-box, in which repose the
" Ouis " which made Louis Napoleon an Emperor, and with
the other to the corpses on the battlefield where the sun of his
empire finally sets. " This," she cries, " has killed that."
The same idea suggested a somewhat similar cartoon, in
which a French peasant, gazing at the shell-battered ruins of

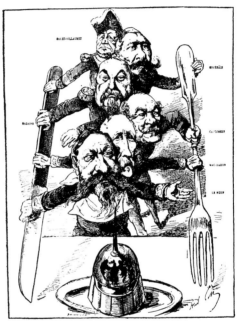

"LET US EAT THE PRUSSIAN."
By André Gill.

his humble home, exclaims in the peasant's ungrammatical
patois: " And it was for this that I voted ' Yes.' " Still
more grim and ominous is the cartoon showing a huge mouse-
trap with three holes. The mouse-trap represents the Plebi-
scite. Two of the holes, marked respectively, " 1851 " and
" 1870," have been sprung, and each has caught the throat of
a victim. The third, however, still yawns open warningly,
with the date not completely filled in.

Still another cartoon, thoroughly characteristic of Daumier's later manner, is "The Dream of Bismarck," one which touches upon the idea which has been used allegorically in connection with every great conqueror whose wake is marked by the strewn corpses of fallen thousands. In it Bismarck, frightfully haggard and ghastly of countenance, is sleeping in his chair, while at his side is the grim figure of Death bearing a huge sickle and pointing out over the bloody battlefield.

Of the younger group of cartoonists none is more closely connected with the events of the *année terrible* than "Cham," the Comte de Noë. The name Noë, it will be remembered, is French for Noah, just as Cham is the French equivalent of Ham, second son of the patriarch of Scripture. The Comte de Noë was also second son of his father, hence the appropriateness of his pseudonym. As a caricaturist, Cham was animated by no such seriousness of purpose as formed the inspiration of Daumier; and this was why he never became a really great caricaturist. It was the humorous side of life, even of the tragedies of life, that appealed to him, and he reflected it back with an incisive drollery which was irresistible. He was one of the most rapid and industrious of workers, and found in the events of *l'année terrible* the inspiration of a vast number of cartoons. The looting propensities of the Prussians were satirized in a sketch showing two Prussian officers looking greedily at a clock on the mantelpiece in a French château. "Let us take the clock." "But peace has already been signed." "No matter. Don't you see the clock is slow?" The German acquisition of the Rhenish provinces is summed up in a picture which shows a German officer attaching to his leg a chain, at the end of which is a huge ball marked Alsace. The siege having

NEW DESIGN FOR A HAND BELL PROPOSED BY "CHARIVARI" FOR THE PUR-
POSE OF REMINDING THE ASSEMBLY THAT PRUSSIAN TROOPS STILL HOLD
FRENCH TERRITORY.
By Daumier.

turned every Parisan into a nominal soldier, this condition of
affairs is hit off by Cham in a cartoon underneath which is
written: "Everybody being soldiers, the officers will have
the right to put through the paces anyone whom they meet in
the streets." The sketch shows a cook in the usual culinary
costume, and bearing on his head a flat basket filled with
kettles and pans, marking time at the command of an officer.
The attitude of England during the war seemed to the caricaturist perfidious, after the practical aid which France had
rendered Albion in the Crimea. Cham hits this off by

representing the two nations as women, Britannia looking ironically at prostrate France and saying: " Oh, no! Prussia has not yet entirely killed her! So it is not yet time to go to her aid."

The statesmen and warriors of that period were very happily caricatured in a series of cartoons, most of which appeared in *L'Eclipse*. Gill excelled in his caricature of

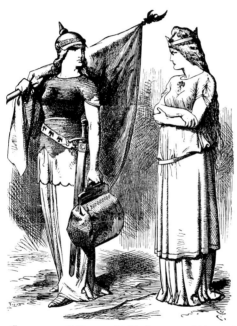

Germany : " Farewell, Madame, and if——
France : " Ha ! We shall meet again !"

individual men rather than in the caricature of events or groups. His real name was Louis Alexandre Gosset. He was born at Landouzy-li-Ville, October 19, 1840, and died in Paris, December 29, 1885. Thiers, Gambetta, Louis Blanc, all the men of the time, were hit off by his pencil. His method in most cases consisted of the grotesque exaggeration of the subject's head at the expense of the body. He was

PILORI-PHRENOLOGIE.

BISMARKOFF 1ᴱ.

Ce masque libéral, trempé d'Hypocrisie,
De sang Républicain prépare une Ambroisie
Pour les rois alliés. Diplomate entêté,
Par la mort et la Honte il frappe Liberté!!!

BISMARCK THE FIRST.

especially happy in his caricature of Thiers, whose diminutive
size, as well as his great importance, made him a favorite
subject for the cartoonist. Thiers as Hamlet soliloquizing,
" To be or not to be "; Thiers as " The Man Who Laughs ";
the head of Thiers peering over the rim of a glass, " A
tempest in a glass of water "; Thiers as the first conscript of
France; Thiers as Achilles in retreat—all these and countless others are from the pencil of Gill.

A striking satirical sketch by Hadol, entitled " La Parade,"
sums up all the buffooneries of the Second Empire. In it

TROCHU—1870.

the Duc de Morny as the barking showman is violently invit-
ing the populace to enter and inspect the wonders of the
Théâtre Badinguet.   Badinguet, as said before, was the
name of the workman in whose clothes Louis Napoleon was
said to have escaped from his imprisonment at Ham; and
throughout the Second Empire it was the name by which the
Parisians maliciously alluded to the Emperor.   Behind De

BAZAINE.
By Faustin.

Morny in the cartoon are the Emperor and Empress, seated
at the cashier's desk at the entrance of the theater to take in
the money of the dupes whom De Morny can persuade to
enter.   To the right and left, in grotesque attire, are the
actors of the show, representing the various statesmen and
soldiers whose names were connected with the reign.

Popular hatred of Marshal Bazaine after the surrender of
Metz, based on the prevalent belief that he had sold the city

and the army under his command to the Germans, finds
pictorial expression in the grim cartoon by Faustin, reproduced here. The artist has cunningly drawn into the features
of the Marshal an expression of unutterable craft and
treachery.   Round his neck there has been flung what at the
first glance seems like a decoration of honor, an impression
strengthened by the cross and inscription on his breast.   But
as you look more closely you perceive that this decoration is
suspended from the noose of the hangman's rope, and that

the words " Au Maréchal Bazaine—La France Reconnais-
sante " have another and a deeper significance. The de-
fender of the city of Paris, General Trochu, was genially
caricatured by André Gill in *L'Eclipse* as a *blanchisseuse*
industriously ironing out the dirty linen of France.   However great his popularity was at the time, Trochu has by no
means escaped subsequent criticism.   To him the resistance
of Paris seemed nothing but " an heroic folly," and he had

ENTRÉE SOLENNELLE DE L'EMPEREUR D'ALLEMAGNE A PARIS

(Caricature de Félix Régamey.)

no hesitation about proclaiming his opinion. Another exceedingly happy caricature by André Gill was that representing Henri Rochefort, the implacable enemy of Louis
Napoleon, as a member of the Government of the National
Defense. Here Rochefort's head is shown peering out of
the mouth of a cannon projecting through a hole in the city's
fortifications.

PART IV

THE END OF THE CENTURY

CHAPTER XXIII

THE EVOLUTION OF AMERICAN CARICATURE

DURING the period covered by the present chapter the foundation of the two leading American comic weeklies, *Puck* and *Judge,* the former in 1877 and the latter in 1881, led to a distinct advance in political caricature in this country. It also made it possible for the first time to draw an intelligent comparison between the tendencies of caricature in England and in America. No one can look over the early files of *Puck* and *Judge* and compare them with *Punch* for the corresponding years without being struck with the contrast, not merely in methods of drawing and printing, but in the whole underlying spirit. For the past half century *Punch* has adhered faithfully to its original attitude of neutrality upon questions of party politics. Its aim has been to represent the weight of public opinion in a sober and conservative spirit; to discountenance and rebuke the excesses of whichever party is in power; to commemorate the great national calamities, as well as the occasions of national rejoicings. If it somewhat overstepped its established bounds in its repeated attacks upon Lord Beaconsfield because his foreign policy was regarded with distrust, it made amends with an eloquent tribute at the time of that statesman's death. And if on one occasion it cartooned him in the guise of the melancholy Dane, with broad impartiality it

231

travestied his great rival, Gladstone, a month or two later, in precisely the same character. Taken as a whole, the English cartoons are not so distinctly popular in tone as those in this country. The underlying thought is apt to be more cultured, more bookish, so to speak; to take the form of parodies upon Shakespere and Dante, Dickens and Scott. And yet, taking them all in all, it would be difficult to point out any parallel series of cartoons which, after the lapse of years, require so little explanation to make them intelligible, or which cover

CARAN D'ACHE.

in so comprehensive a manner the current history of the world.

On the other hand, the typical American cartoon of a generation ago concerned itself but little with questions of international interest, while in its treatment of domestic affairs it was largely lacking in the dignity and restraint which characterized the British school. Being founded upon party politics, its purpose was primarily not to reflect public opinion, but to mold it; to make political capital; to win votes by fair means, if possible, but to win them. From their very inception *Puck* and *Judge,* as the mouthpieces of their respective parties, have exerted a formidable power, whose far-reaching influence it would be impossible to gauge, especially during the febrile periods of the Presidential campaigns. At these times the animosity shown in some of the cartoons seems rather surprising, when looked at from the sober vantage ground of later years. Political molehills were exaggerated into mountains, and even those elements of vulgar vitupera-

GULLIVER CRISPI.
From "*Il Papagallo*" (Rome).

tion and cheap personal abuse—features of political campaigns which we are happily outgrowing—were eagerly seized upon for the purpose of pictorial satire. The peculiar bitterness which marked the memorable campaign between Mr. Cleveland and Mr. Blaine in 1884 was strongly mirrored in the political caricature of the time. It marked the highwater line of the element of purely personal abuse in comic art. In the end the extreme measures to which each

Fig. 291. — Caricature de Gill. (*Éclipse*, 19 octobre 1873.)

of the rival parties resorted during that year had very
beneficial effects, for after the election the nation, in calmer
mood, grew ashamed at the thought of its violence and
bitterness, and subsequent campaigns have consequently been
much more free from these objectionable features.   Mr.
Harrison, Mr. Bryan, Mr. McKinley, and Mr. Roosevelt
have all been assailed from many different points.   But we
are no longer in the mood to tolerate attempts to rake up

alleged personal scandals and to use them in the pamphlet and the cartoon. Enough of this was done by both parties in 1884 to last us for at least a generation. There are cartoons which appeared in *Puck* and *Judge* which even at this day we should not think of reprinting, and which the publications containing them and the artists who drew them would probably like to forget.

Nevertheless, to the close student of political history there is in the American cartoon of this period, with all its flamboyant colorings, its reckless exaggeration, its puerile animosity, material which the more sober and dignified British cartoon does not offer. It does not sum up so adequately the sober second thought of the nation, but it does keep us in touch with the changing mood of popular opinion, its varying pulse-beat from hour to hour. To glance over the old files throughout any one of the Presidential campaigns is the next best thing to living them over again, listening once more to the daily heated arguments, the inflammable stump speeches, the rancorous vituperation which meant so much at the time, and which seemed so idle the day after the election.

CHAPTER XXIV

IT is not strange that during these years American cartoonists concerned themselves but little with matters outside of their own country. For more than a decade after the close of the Franco-Prussian War there were very few episodes which assumed international importance, and still fewer in which the United States had any personal interest. France was amply occupied in recovering from the effects of her exhaustive struggle; United Germany was undergoing the process of crystallizing into definite form. Europe, as a whole, had no more energy than was needed to attend to domestic affairs and to keeping a jealous eye upon English ambition in Egypt and Russian aggression in the Balkan States. For some little time after the French Commune echoes of that internecine struggle were still to be found in the work of caricaturists, both in France and Germany. Before taking final leave of that veteran French artist, Honoré Daumier, it seems necessary to allude briefly to a few of the cartoons of that splendidly tragic series of his old age dealing with the France which, having undergone the horrors of the Germanic invasion and of the Commune, is shattered but not broken, and begins to look forward with wistful eyes to a time when she shall have recovered her strength and her prosperity. One of the most striking of these cartoons represents France as a deep-rooted tree which has been bent and rent by the passing whirlwind. " Poor France! The branches are broken, but the trunk holds always." Simple as

"POOR FRANCE! THE BRANCHES ARE BROKEN, BUT THE TRUNK STILL HOLDS."
By Daumier in "Charivari."

the design is, the artist by countless touches of light and of
shadow has given it a somber significance which long remains
in the memory.   It was to Napoleon that Daumier bitterly
ascribed the misfortunes of *La Patrie,* and in these cartoons
he lost no opportunity of attacking Napoleonic legend.
Stark and dead, nailed to the Book of History is the Imperial
eagle.   " You will remain outside, nailed fast on the cover,

a hideous warning to future generations of Frenchmen," is Daumier's moral.   Of brighter nature is the cartoon called

"You shall stay there, nailed to the cover, a warning to future generations of Frenchmen."
By Daumier in " Charivari."

" The New Year."   It represents the dawning of 1872, and portrays France sweeping away the last broken relics of her period of disaster.

In Germany, also, one finds a few tardy cartoons bearing upon Napoleon III.   Even in the *Fliegende Blätter,* a periodical which throughout its history has confined itself, with few exceptions, to social satire, perennial skits upon the dignified Herr Professor, the self-important young lieutenant, the punctilious university student, one famous cartoon appeared late in the year 1871, entitled " The Root of All Evil."   It portrayed Napoleon III., as a gigantic, distorted vegetable of the carrot or turnip order, his flabby features distended into tuberous rotundity, the familiar hall-mark of his sweeping mustache and imperial lengthened grotesquely

into the semblance of a threefold root.   Still better known
is a series of cartoons which ran through half a dozen numbers of the *Fliegende Blätter,* entitled " The Franco-Prussian
War: A Tragedy in Five Acts," in which the captions are all
clever applications of lines from Schiller's "Maid of Orleans.
As compared with the work of really great cartoonists, this
series has little to make it memorable.   But as an expression
of a victorious nation's good-natured contempt, its tendency

THE NEW YEAR BRINGS NEW HOPE FOR FRANCE.
By Daumier in "Charivari."

to view the whole fierce struggle of 1870-71 as an amusing
farce enacted by a company of grotesque marionettes, it is
not without significance and interest.

Almost as Germanic in sentiment and in execution as the
" Maid of Orleans " series in the *Fliegende Blätter* was the
curious little volume entitled " The Fight at Dame Europa's
School," written and illustrated by Thomas Nast.   This skit,
which was printed in New York after the close of the War,

contained thirty-three drawings which are remarkable chiefly in that they are comparatively different from anything else that Nast ever did and bear a striking resemblance to the war cartoons of the German papers. The Louis Napoleon of this book is so much like the Louis Napoleon of the *Fliegende Blätter* that one is bound to feel that one was the

" THE ROOT OF ALL EVIL.
From the " Fliegende Blätter" in 1871.

The whole spirit of these pictures, which appeared in the *Fliegende Blätter* after the Napoleonic downfall in 1871, is a travesty on the splendid lines of Schiller in the "Maid of Orleans" (Jungfrau von Orleans).

direct inspiration of the other. The text of the book, though nothing astonishing, serves its purpose in elucidating the drawings. It tells of the well-ordered educational establishment kept by Dame Europa in which the five largest boys acted as monitors, to keep the unruly pupils in order. These boys were Louis, William, Aleck, Joseph, and John. If a dispute arose among any of the smaller boys, the monitors had to examine into its cause, and, if possible, to settle it amicably. Should it be necessary to fight the matter out, they were to see fair play, stop the encounter when it had gone far enough, and at all times to uphold justice, and to prevent tyranny and bullying. In this work Master Louis and Master John were particularly prominent. There was a tradition in the school of a terrific row in times past, when a monitor named Nicholas attacked a very dirty little boy called Constantine. John and Louis pitched in, and gave Nicholas such a thrashing that he never got over it, and soon afterward left the school. Now each of the upper boys had a little garden of his own in which he took great pride and interest. In the center of each garden there was an arbor, fitted up according to the taste and means of its owner. Louis had the prettiest arbor of all, while that of John was a mere tool-house. When the latter wished to enjoy a holiday he would punt himself across the brook and enjoy himself in the arbor of his friend Louis. By the side of Louis's domain was that of William, who, though proud of his own garden, never went to work in it without casting an envious glance on two little flower beds which now belonged to Louis, but which ought by rights he thought to belong to him. Over these flower beds he often talked with his favorite fag, a shrewd lad named Mark, full of deep tricks and dodges.

"There is only one way to do it," said Mark. "If you

Fig. 294. — La situation politique en France. (Novembre 1873.)

Caricature de Felix Régamey, publiée dans le *Harper's Weekley* de New-York.

want the flower beds, you must fight Louis for them, and I believe you will lick him all to smash; but you must fight him alone."

" How do you mean? " replied William.

" I mean, you must take care that the other monitors don't interfere in the quarrel. If they do, they will be sure to go against you. Remember what a grudge Joseph owes you for the licking you gave him not along ago; and Aleck, though to be sure Louis took little Constantine's part against him in that great bullying row, is evidently beginning to grow jealous of your influence in the school. You see, old fellow, you have grown so much lately, and filled out so wonderfully that you are getting really quite formidable. Why, I recollect the time when you were quite a little chap! "

Thereupon the astute Mark designs a plan by which William may provoke the encounter while making Louis seem the aggressor. And so on, under the guise of fist-fight between two schoolboys, Nast tells of all the events of the struggle of 1871; the outbreak of hostilities, the Baptism of Fire, Sedan, the German march on Paris, the Siege, and the different attitudes assumed by the other monitors.

CHAPTER XXV

GENERAL EUROPEAN AFFAIRS

PUNCH, however, is really the most satisfactory and comprehensive source for the history of political caricature during the years following the siege of Paris down to 1886. From the indefatigable pencil of Tenniel and Sambourne we get an exhaustive and pungent record of the whole period of Disraeli's ascendency, the fruits

"NEW CROWNS FOR OLD."
Disraeli offering Victoria the Imperial crown
of India.

of his much-criticised foreign policy, England's attitude regarding the Suez Canal, her share in the Turco-Russian conflict, her acquisition of the island of Cyprus, the fall of Khartoum, the Fenian difficulties of 1885, and the history of Mr. Gladstone's Home Rule policy.

Throughout the cartoons of this period there is no one figure which appears with more persistent regularity than

" TIGHTENING THE GRIP."

that of Lord Beaconsfield, and with scarcely an exception he is uniformly treated with an air of indulgent contempt. Of course, his strongly marked features, the unmistakably Semitic cast of nose and lips, the closely curled black ringlets clustering above his ears, all offered irresistible temptation to the cartoonist, with the result that throughout the entire series, in whatever guise he is portrayed, the suggestion of charlatan, of necromancer, of mountebank, of one kind or another of the endless genus " fake," is never wholly absent.

Even in Tenniel's cartoon, "New Crowns for Old," which commemorates the passage of the Royal Titles Bill, conferring upon the Queen the title of Empress of India, the scene is confessedly adapted from Aladdin, and "Dizzy" is portrayed as a slippery Oriental with an oily smile, in the act of trading a gaudy-looking piece of tinsel headgear for the more modest, but genuine, regal crown topped with the cross of Malta. The bestowal of the title of Earl of Beaconsfield upon Mr. Disraeli, which followed within a very few weeks, was too good a chance for satire for Mr. Tenniel to let pass, and he hit it off in a page entitled "One Good Turn Deserves Another," in which Victoria, with the Imperial crown of India upon her head, is conferring a coronet upon "Dizzy," kneeling obsequiously at her feet.

At this time the one international question which bade fair to assume any considerable importance was that of Russia's attitude in the Balkan peninsula. Already in June, 1886,

ÆOLUS—RULER OF THE STORMS. THE EASTERLY
WIND TOO MUCH FOR BISMARCK.

we find *Punch* portraying the Czar of Russia as a master of the hounds, just ready to let slip the leash from his "dogs of war," Servia, Montenegro, Bosnia, and Herzegovina, in pur-

suit of the unsuspecting Sultan of Turkey, while John Bull
in the guise of a policeman, is cautiously peering from behind
a fence, evidently wondering whether this is a case which calls
for active interference.   It is only a few days later that the

" L'ÉTAT C'EST MOI! "

outbreak of an insurrection in Bosnia and Herzegovina
hastens a decision on the part of Europe to " keep the Ring "
and let the Sultan ward off the " dogs of war " single-handed
—an incident duly commemorated in *Punch* on June 19.
The Turkish atrocities in Bulgaria, however, aroused public
sentiment throughout the Continent to such a degree that the
Powers united in demanding an armistice. Tenniel's interpretation of this incident takes the form of a sick-chamber, in
which the Sick Man of Europe is surrounded by a corps of
illustrious physicians, Drs. Bull, William I., Francis Joseph
and Company, who are firmly insisting that their patient shall

swallow a huge pill labeled " Armistice "—" or else there's
no knowing what might happen ! " The protocol on Turkish affairs which soon after this was proposed by Russia and
supported by Disraeli, forms the subject of two suggestive
cartoons in *Punch*. The first, entitled " Pons Asinorum,"
depicts the protocol as a make-shift bridge supported on the
docile shoulders of John Bull and the other European Powers, and spanning a lagoon entitled " Eastern Question."

THE HIDDEN HAND.

Over this bridge the Russian bear is stealthily crawling to
his desired goal, his eye half closed in a sly wink,
his sides bristling like a veritable arsenal with
weapons. The second cartoon, alluding to the Porte's re-
jection of the protocol, represents Disraeli looking disconsolately upon a smoldering pile of powder kegs and ammu-

nition, over which he has placed the protocol, twisted into
the shape of a candle-snuffer. "Confound the thing! It
is all ablaze!" he ejaculates, while Lord Hartington reminds him, "Ah, my dear D., paper will burn, you know!"

The next significant caricature in the *Punch* series belongs
to the period of actual hostilities between Turkey and Russia, after Plevna had been completely invested and the Turks
were at all points being steadily beaten back. This caricature, entitled "Tightening the Grip," showing the strug-
gling Turk being slowly crushed to death in the relentless

THE IRISH FRANKENSTEIN.

hug of the gigantic bear, may safely be left to speak for
itself without further description. Meanwhile, England
was watching with growing disquiet Russia's actions in the
Balkans. In one cartoon of this period, Mr. Bull is bluntly
refusing to be drawn into a game of "Blind Hookey" with

the other European Powers. " Now then, Mr. Bull, we're
only waiting for you," says Russia; and John Bull rejoins:
" Thank you, I don't like the game. I like to see the cards! "
Prince Bismarck at this time was doing his best to bring about
an understanding between England and Russia, but the difficulties of the situation threatened to prove too much even
for that veteran diplomat. *Punch* cleverly hit off the situation by representing Bismarck as Æolus, the wind-god, strug-
gling desperately with an unmanageable wind-bag, which is
swelling threateningly in the direction of the East and assuming the form of a dangerous war-cloud. Eventually all mis-
understandings were peacefully smoothed away at the Berlin
Congress, which Tenniel commemorates with a cartoon showing " Dizzy " in the guise of a tight-rope performer triumphantly carrying the Sultan on his shoulders along a rope
labeled " Congress," his inherent double-dealing being sug-

THE DARING DUCKLING. JUNE, 1883.
An early appearance of Mr. Chamberlain in
caricature.

gested by his balancing pole, which he sways back and forth
indifferently, and the opposite ends of which are labeled
" peace " and " war."

Comparatively few cartoons of this period touch upon

American matters. All the more noteworthy is the one
which Mr. Tenniel dedicated to the memory of President
Garfield at the time of the latter's assassination. It is a
worthy example of the artist's most serious manner, at once
dignified and impressive. It bears the inscription, " A Common Sorrow," and shows a weeping Columbia clasped closely
in the arms of a sorrowing and sympathetic Britannia.

SETTLING THE ALABAMA CLAIMS.

M. Gambetta seldom received attention at the hands of
English caricaturists; but in 1881, when the resignation of
Jules Ferry and his colleagues resulted in the formation of a
new ministry with Gambetta at the head, and both English
and German newspapers were sarcastically saying that " the
Gambetta Cabinet represented only himself," *Punch* had to
have his little fling at the French statesman, portraying him
as beaming with self-complacence, and striking an attitude

in front of a statue of Louis XIV., while he echoes the latter's
famous dictum, " L'Etat c'est moi ! "

Two cartoons which tell their own story are devoted to
Fenianism. The first commemorates the Phœnix Park out-
rage in which Lord Frederick Cavendish, the newly appointed
Chief Secretary, lost his life. The cartoon is called " The
Irish Frankenstein," and is certainly baleful enough to do full

" MIRAGE!
GORDON WAITING AT KHARTOUM.

justice to the hideousness of the crime it is intended to sym-
bolize. The second cartoon, entitled " The Hidden Hand,"
shows the Fenian monster receiving a bag of gold from a
mysterious hand stretched from behind a curtain. The reference is to a supposed inner circle of assassins, directed and
paid by greater villains who kept themselves carefully behind the scenes.

The tragedy of Khartoum formed the subject of several

grim and forceful pages. " Mirage " was almost prophetic in its conception, representing General Gordon gazing across the desert, where, by the tantalizing refraction of the air, he can plainly see the advancing British hosts, which in reality are destined to arrive too late. " Too late," in fact, are the very words which serve as a caption of the next cartoon. Khartoum has fallen, and Britannia, having come upon a fruitless mission, stands a picture of despair, her face buried upon her arm, her useless shield lying neglected upon the ground.

CHAPTER XXVI

THOMAS NAST

IT was not until late in the '60's, when Thomas Nast began his pictorial campaign in the pages of *Harper's Weekly* against the Ring which held New York in its clutches, that American caricature could claim a pencil which entitled it to any sort of consideration from the artistic point of view. Some of the cartoons which have been reproduced in earlier papers of this series have possessed unquestionable cleverness of invention and idea; for instance, many of those dealing with President Jackson's administration and his relations with the United States Bank, and some of the purely allegorical cartoons treating of slavery and of the Civil War. But in all these there was so much lacking; so many artistic shortcomings were covered up by the convenient loops. The artists felt themselves free from any obligation to give expression to the countenances of their subjects so long as the fundamental idea was there, and the loops offered an easy vehicle for the utterance of thoughts and feelings which a modern artist would feel obliged to express in the drawing itself—by a skillful quirk of the pencil, an added line, an exaggerated smile or frown. It was a thoroughly wooden school of caricature, in which one can find no trace of the splendid suggestion which the caricaturists should at that time have been drawing from contemporary masters of the art in France and England.

Although during the years of his fecundity Thomas Nast drew many cartoons bearing on events of international importance, his name will always be remembered, first of all, in connection with the series through which he held up the extravagances and iniquities of the Tweed Ring in the pillory of public opinion. He had decided convictions on other subjects. To the end of his life it was his nature to feel intensely, even in small matters. But his scorn and hatred of the corrupt organization that was looting New York became a positive mania, which was reflected in the cartoons which he literally hurled week after week against Tweed and his satellites. "I don't care what they write about me," said

THE GRATZ BROWN TAG TO GREELEY'S COAT.

Tweed, " but can't you stop those terrible cartoons?" and in the end they, more than anything else, led to his downfall, his flight and his capture in Spain, where he was recognized

THOMAS NAST.

by the police through the likeness Nast had drawn of him as
a kidnaper.   But in recognizing Nast's services in behalf
of New York City it is not fair to overlook his work as a

FIRST APPEARANCE OF THE CAP AND DINNER PAIL
AS EMBLEMATIC OF LABOR.

political caricaturist on broader issues.   To him we owe also
the Gratz Brown tag to Greeley's coat in the campaign of
1872, the " Rag Baby of Inflation," the Jackass as emblematic of the Democratic Party, the Labor Cap and the Full
Dinner Pail, which in later years were so much developed
by the cartoonists of *Judge*. And if to-day, at the beginning of
the twentieth century, we have a school of caricature which
for scope and craftsmanship is equal, if not superior, to that
of any nation of Europe, it is only just to recognize that it
was Thomas Nast who first gave American caricature a dignity and a meaning.

The earliest Presidential election which falls within the scope of the present chapter, that of 1872, antedates the establishment of American comic weeklies. The central figure in the few caricatures which have survived from that year was, of course, Horace Greeley, whose candidacy at one time was thought seriously to threaten the fortunes of the Republican Party. The caricatures themselves, with the exception of those drawn by Thomas Nast, show little improvement over the caricatures which were executed during the Civil War. The artists relied entirely upon the traditional loops to make them intelligible to the public, and the features of the political characters portrayed were expressionless and wooden. One of the best of this series was drawn in support of the Horace Greeley candidacy. Uncle Sam is represented as a landlord and President Grant as his tenant, a shiftless

THE FIRST "RAG BABY."

widow with a dog at her heels and a bottle of rum in the basket on her arm. The Widow Grant has come to ask for a new lease. "Well, Uncle Sam," she says, "I've called to see if you will let me have the White House for four years

longer, as I find the place suits me very well." " No, Marm
Grant," retorts Uncle Sam, shaking his head, " I reckon I'll
do no such thing. I've had too many complaints about you
from the neighbors during the last four years. I'm just sick
of you and your tobacco smoke and bull pups, so I've given

THE DONKEY.   FIRST USED TO RIDICULE THE IN-
FLATION TENDENCY.

the lease to Honest Horace Greeley, who will take better care
of the place than you have."

In another of this series Horace Greeley is represented as
the entering wedge that is splitting the rock of the Republican
Party. Greeley, with a paper bearing the words " Free
Trade " in one hand and one bearing " Protection " in the
other, is being hammered into the cleft in the Republican
rock by a huge mallet—Democratic Nomination—wielded
by Carl Schurz. " This is rather a novel position for a
stanch old Republican like me," he says. " I begin to feel
as if I was in a tight place." President Grant, with a cigar
in his hand, is looking on complacently. " My friend," he

calls out to Schurz, " you've got a soft thing on your wedge, but your mallet will kill the man." To which Schurz replies: " I don't care who's killed, if we succeed in defeating your election." Below, creeping furtively about the rock, are the figures of Dana, Sumner, Gratz Brown, Trumbull, Hall, Sweeny, Tweed, and Hoffman of the Ring. " Anything to beat Grant!" is the cry of these conspirators. " Honesty is the word to shout, there are so many rogues about," mutters Tweed. " Oh, how freely we'll win with Greeley," says Hall. " Anything to beat Grant. He wouldn't make me Collector for New York," are the words of Dana. The cartoon is a belated specimen of the school of American caricature which was in vogue in the days of President Jackson.

As has already been stated, *Puck* was not founded until 1877, too late to take part in the Tilden-Hayes campaign. When we speak of *Puck,* however, we refer, of course, to the

THE BRAINS OF TAMMANY.

edition printed in English, for, as a matter of fact, twenty-four numbers of a German *Puck* were published during the year 1876.

As that year was an important one in American history, these numbers can by no means be ignored, and despite their

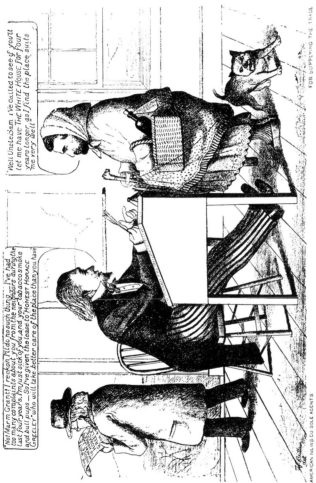

"A POPULAR VERDICT."

TAYLOR&CO. PUBLISHERS, NEW YORK.

AMERICAN NEWS CO. SOLE AGENTS

FOR SUPPLYING THE TRADE

crude appearance when contrasted with the *Puck* of later days, they contain some of Keppler's most admirable work. For instance, there is the figure of the tattooed Columbia, the precursor of Gillam's famous Tattooed Man. This figure ap-

THE TATTOOED COLUMBIA.
By courtesy of the Puck Company.

peared in November, 1876, and was the idea of Charles Hauser, a member of the first editorial staff of the young weekly. The artist's idea of the unhappy condition of our nation is shown in the hideous tattooed designs with which Columbia's body is scarred from head to foot. We can read " Whisky Ring," " Black Friday," " Secession," " Tammany," " Election Frauds," " Corruption," " Civil War," " Credit Mobilier," and " Taxes." The figure is as repulsive as that which eight years later drove Mr. Blaine to frenzy.

From the Collection of the New York Historical Society.

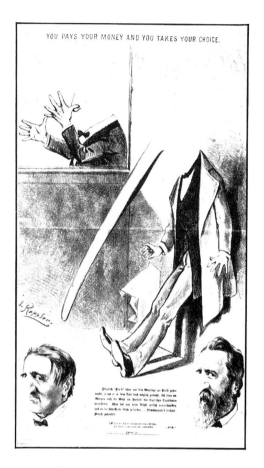

A familiar device in the caricature of the later '70's was that of representing political figures as being headless and placing their heads in another part of the picture, so that you might adjust them to suit yourself. In this way the artist did not commit himself to prophecy and was enabled to please both parties. For instance, an excellent example of this is shown in the cartoon called " You Pays Your Money and You Takes Your Choice," drawn by Keppler during the

From the collection of the New York Historical Society.

campaign of 1876. Of the two headless figures one is seated in the window of the White House gesticulating derisively at his beaten opponent. The other, thoroughly crushed and with a nose of frightfully exaggerated length—both Mr. Tilden and Mr. Hayes were rather large-nosed men—is leaning helplessly against the wall of the cold outside. At the bottom of the picture are the heads of the two candidates, which one might cut out and adjust as pleased himself.

CHAPTER XXVII

PROBABLY no cartoon dealing with the Garfield-Hancock campaign of 1880 was more widely discussed than that called " Forbidding the Banns," drawn for *Puck* by Keppler. It was a cartoon which an American comic paper would publish to-day only after considerable hesitation, for there was in it the spirit of a less delicate age, a coarseness which was pardonable only when the genuine strength and humor of the complete work are taken into consideration. " Forbidding the Banns " shows a political wedding party at the altar with Uncle Sam as the reluctant and uncomfortable groom, General Garfield as the eager bride, and the figure of the ballot box as the officiating clergyman. The bridesmaids are Mr. Whitelaw Reid and Carl Schurz, with Murat Halstead bringing up the rear. The ceremony is well along and the contracting parties are about to be united when W. H. Barnum, the chairman of the Democratic National Committee, rushes in shouting, " I forbid the banns! " and waving frantically the figure of a little baby marked " Credit Mobilier." The faces of all the bridal party show consternation at the unexpected interruption, while the bride protests coyly: " But it was such a little one."

The defeat of General Hancock in 1880 was commemorated by Keppler in *Puck* with the cartoon called " The Wake over the Remains of the Democratic Party." The ludicrous corpse of the defunct is stretched on a rough board

"FORBIDDING THE BANNS." A FAMOUS CARTOON OF THE GARFIELD-HANCOCK CAMPAIGN.

By courtesy of the Puck Company.

and covered with a loose sheet. The lighted candles at the four corners protrude from the necks of bottles, and the mourners are indulging in a protracted carouse which seems destined to end in a free fight. In the center of the picture Kelly, with Ben Butler as a partner, is doing a dance in the most approved manner of Donnybrook Fair. All about there is the general atmosphere of turmoil and unnatural excitement, but the figures of Hewitt, Davis, Belmont, and English are stretched out in a manner indicating that the festivities of the night have proved too much for them.

As has already been pointed out, the political caricature commemorating the Cleveland-Blaine campaign of 1884 was chiefly remarkable for its extraordinary rancor. There was little, if any, really good-natured satire underlying these cartoons; they were designed and executed vindictively, and their main object was to hurt. Mr. Cleveland's official record in Buffalo, and as Governor of New York, had been such as to cause many of the more liberal Republicans to support his candidacy and offered little to the political cartoonist, so the opponents of Republican caricature found it expedient to base their attacks on matters of purely personal nature.

Even in later years the cartoonist did not entirely refrain from this method of belittling Mr. Cleveland's capabilities. It was sneeringly said that much of the success of his administration was due to the charm, the tact, and the personal magnetism of Mrs. Cleveland, and this idea was the inspiration of a number of cartoons which were far from being in the best of taste. One of these which was not particularly offensive was that entitled " Mr. Cleveland's Best Card." It was simply a huge playing card bearing the picture of Mrs. Cleveland. Another much more obnoxious was a curious imitation of the famous French cartoon " Partant pour la

THE WAKE OVER THE REMAINS OF THE DEMOCRATIC PARTY AFTER THE ELECTION OF 1880.

By courtesy of the Puck Company.

A COMMON SORROW.

Syrie," which was published in Paris after the flight of the
Empress Eugénie.

The Democratic cartoonists, besides their use of the Tattooed Man idea and the alleged scandals in Mr. Blaine's
political career, made a strong point of the soundness and
cleanness of Mr. Cleveland's official record. A typical caricature of this nature was that drawn by Gillam called " Why
They Dislike Him." It represents Mr. Cleveland as a lion
lying on the rock of Civil Service Reform. Perched on the
limb of a tree overhead are a group of chattering monkeys,
his political enemies, who are hurling at him imprecations
and abuse because he will not consent to serve as the cats-
paw to pluck the chestnuts for them out of the political fire.

WHY THEY DISLIKE HIM.

By courtesy of the Puck Company.

THE FIRST "TATTOOED MAN" CARTOON

By courtesy of the Puck Company.

Familiar faces among the group of noisy bandar-log are those of Croker, Butler, and Dana. Prostrate and helpless under the paw of the lion is a monkey with the face of Grady.

The most terrible and effective series of cartoons published during the Cleveland-Blaine campaign was that in which the Republican candidate appeared as the Tattooed Man in the political show. For many weeks during the summer and autumn of 1884 Mr. Blaine was assailed through this figure in the pages of *Puck*. The story of the origin of this historic cartoon is as follows: Mr. Bernard Gillam, the artist, had conceived the idea of a cartoon in which each of the Presidential possibilities should appear as some sort of freak in a political side-show. One of these freaks was to be the Tattooed Man, but Mr. Gillam at first hit upon David Davis as the person to be so represented. He was describing the proposed cartoon one day in the office of *Puck* when Mr. Bunner, who was at that time the editor, turned suddenly and said: "David Davis? Nonsense! Blaine is the man for that." The cartoon so conceived was splendidly executed, and became one of the great pictorial factors in turning the scale of the election. It stirred Mr. Blaine himself to a point where he resolved to prosecute the publishers of *Puck,* and was persuaded from this course only by the very strongest pressure. The tattoo marks which were most obnoxious to him were those which spelled out the word " Bribery." A curious feature of this series was that Mr. Bernard Gillam was an ardent Republican, voting for Mr. Blaine on election day, and at the same time that he was executing the Tattooed Man cartoon in *Puck* was suggesting equally vindictive caricatures of Mr. Cleveland and the Democratic party for the rival pages of *Judge.*

CHAPTER XXVIII

IN looking backward over a century of caricature, it is interesting to ask just what it is that makes the radical difference between the cartoon of to-day and that of a hundred years ago. That there is a wide gulf between the comparative restraint of the modern cartoonist and the unbridled license of Gillray's or Rowlandson's grotesque, gargoyle types, is self-evident; that comic art, as applied to politics, is to-day more widespread, more generally appreciated, and in a quiet way more effective in molding public opinion than ever before, needs no argument. And yet, if one stops to analyze the individual cartoons, to take them apart and discover the essence of their humor, the incisive edge of their irony and satire, one finds that there is nothing really new in them; that the basic principles of caricature were all understood as well in the eighteenth century as in the nineteenth, and that, in many cases, the successful cartoon of to-day is simply the replica of an old one of a past generation, modified to fit a new set of facts. When Gilbert Stuart drew his famous " Gerrymander " cartoon, he was probably not the first artist to avail himself of the chance resemblance of the geographical contour of a state or country to some person or animal. He certainly was not the last. Again and again the map of the United States has been drawn so as to bring out some significant similarity, as recently when it was distorted into a ludicrous semblance of Mr. Cleveland, bending low in proud humility, the living embodiment of the

A GERMAN IDEA OF IRISH HOME RULE.

principle, *L'Etat c'est Moi;* or again, just before our war with Spain, when it was so drawn as to present a capital likeness of Uncle Sam, the Atlantic and Gulf States forming his nose and mouth, the latter suggestively opened to take in Cuba, which is swimming dangerously near. *Puck's* famous " Tattooed Man " was only a new application of an idea that had been used before; while the representation of a group of leading politicians as members of a freak show, a circus, or a minstrel troop, is as old as minstrels or dime

3d Edition. 4 A. M.

The World.

3d Edition. 4 A. M.

VOL. XXV., NO. 8,479.

NEW YORK, THURSDAY, NOVEMBER 6, 1884.

PRICE TWO CENTS.

CLEVELAND.

He will Surely be the Next President.

New York, Indiana, New Jersey and Connecticut.

They Stand Solidly and Squarely in the Democratic Column.

Michigan Probably Carried for Blaine.

Wisconsin No Longer Claimed by the Democrats.

Democratic Gains in Illinois, but the State Republican.

Blaine Sure to Stand the Two Virginias and Florida.

But Cleveland has 219 Electoral Votes and will .. President.

THE MAN FOR THE HOUR AND THE OCCASION. THE EMPIRE STATE.

PEACE AND PROSPERITY

PUBLIC OFFICE IS A PUBLIC TRUST

The New National Sexton—"He Gathers Them In."

It is Democratic and Will So Remain.

Gov. Cleveland's Plurality Between 4,000 and 5,000.

The Congressional Delegation Will Be 17 to 17.

The Republicans Still Retain the Assembly.

Decided Democratic Gains Reported From Republican Strongholds.

museums themselves. Few leading statesmen of the past
half century have not at some time in their career been portrayed as Hamlet, or Macbeth, or Richard III.; while as
for the conventional use of animals and symbolic figures to
represent the different nations, the British Lion and the
Russian Bear, Uncle Sam and French Liberty, these belong
to the raw materials of caricature, dating back to its very inception as an art. And yet, while the means used are essentially the same as in the days of Hogarth and Cruikshank,
the results are radically different.

The reason for this difference may be summed up in a
single word—Journalism. The modern cartoon is essentially journalistic, both in spirit and in execution. The spasmodic single sheets of Gillray's period, huge lithographs that

HORATIUS CLEVELAND AT THE BRIDGE.
From New York "Life."

found their way to the public through the medium of London
print shops, were long ago replaced by the weekly comic
papers, while to-day these in turn find formidable rivals in
the cartoons which have become a feature of most of the lead-

ing daily journals. The celerity with which a caricature is
now conceived and executed, thanks to the modern mechanical improvements and the prevailing spirit of alertness,
makes it possible for the cartoonist to keep pace with the
news of the day, to seize upon the latest political blunder, the
social fad of the moment, and hit it off with a stroke of incisive irony, without fear that it will be forgotten before the

BERNARD GILLAM OF "JUDGE."

drawing can appear in print. The consequences of all this
modern haste and enterprise are not wholly advantageous.
Real talent is often wasted upon mediocre ideas under the
compulsion of producing a daily cartoon, and again a really
brilliant conception is marred by overhaste in execution, a
lack of artistic finish in the detail. Besides, the tendency of a
large part of contemporary cartoons is toward the local and

JOSEPH KEPPLER OF " PUCK."

the ephemeral. This is especially true of the caricatures which appear during an American political campaign, in which every petty blunder, every local issue, every bit of personal gossip, is magnified into a vital national principle, a world-wide scandal. And when the morning after the election dawns, the business settles down into its wonted channel, these momentous issues, and the flamboyant cartoons which proclaimed them, suddenly become as trivial and as empty as a spent firecracker or Roman candle.

But another change which the spirit of journalism has wrought in the contemporary cartoon, and a more vital change than any other, is due to the definite editorial policy which lies behind it. The dominant note in all the work of the great cartoonists of the past, in the English Gillray and the French Daumier, was the note of individualism. Take away the personal rancor, the almost irrational hatred of " Little Boney " from Gillray, take away Daumier's mordant irony, his fearless contempt for Louis Philippe, and the life of their work is gone. The typical cartoon of to-day is, to a large extent, not a one-man production at all. It is frequently built up, piecemeal, one detail at a time, and in the case of a journal like *Punch* or *Judge* or *Life* often represents the thoughtful collaboration of the entire staff. In the case of the leading dailies, the cartoon must be in accord with the settled political policy of the paper, as much as the leading articles on the editorial page. The individual preferences of the cartoonist do not count. In fact, he may be doing daily violence to his settled convictions, or he may find means of espousing both sides at once, as was the case with Mr. Gillam, who throughout the Cleveland-Blaine campaign was impartially drawing Democratic cartoons for *Puck* and suggesting Republican cartoons for *Judge* at the same time.

What the political cartoon will become in the future, it is dangerous to predict. There is, however, every indication that its influence, instead of diminishing, is likely to increase steadily. What it has lost in ceasing to be the expression of the individual mind, the impulsive product of erratic genius, it has more than gained in its increased timeliness, its greater sobriety, its more sustained and definite purpose. At certain epochs in the past it has served as a vehicle for reckless scandal-mongering and scurrilous personal abuse. But this it seems to have happily outgrown. That pictorial satire may be made forceful without the sacrifice of dignity was long ago demonstrated by Tenniel's powerful work in the pages of *Punch*. And there is no doubt that a serious political issue, when presented in the form of a telling cartoon, will be borne home to the minds of a far larger circle of average every-day men and women than it ever could be when discussed in the cold black and white of the editorial column.

Another interesting effect of the growing conservative spirit in caricature is seen in the gradual crystallization of certain definite symbolic types. Allusion has already been

THE JOHN BULL OCTOPUS IN EGYPT.
From "Il Papagallo" (Rome).

made, in earlier chapters of this work, to the manner in which the conception of John Bull and Uncle Sam and other analogous types, has been gradually built up by almost imperceptible degrees, each artist preserving all the essential work of his predecessor, and adding a certain indefinable something of his own, until a certain definite portrait has been produced, a permanent ideal, whose characteristic features the

cartoonists of the future could no more alter arbitrarily than
they could the features of Bismarck or Gladstone. And not
only have these crystallized types become accepted by the
nation at large,—not only is Uncle Sam the same familiar
figure, tall and lanky, from the New York *Puck* to the San
Francisco *Wasp,*—but gradually these national types have
migrated and crossed the seas, and to-day they are the com-

A HAND AGAINST EVERY MAN.
From London "Judy," April 13, 1892.

mon property of comic artists of all nations. John Bull and
the Russian Bear, Columbia and the American Eagle, are
essentially the same, whether we meet them in the press of
Canada, Australia, Cape Colony, or the United States. And
for the very reason that there is so little variety in the obvious
features, the mere physical contour, the subtler differences
due to race prejudice and individual limitations are all the

THE STABILITY OF THE TRIPLE ALLIANCE.
From " Il Papagallo" (Rome).

more significant and interesting. There are cases, and comparatively recent cases, too, where race-prejudice has found
expression in such rampant and illogical violence as prompted
many of the Spanish cartoons during our recent war over
Cuba, in which Americans were regularly portrayed as hogs
—big hogs and little hogs, some in hog-pens, others running
at large—but one and all of them as hogs. The cartoonists
of the Continent, Frenchmen, Germans, and Italians alike,
have difficulty in accepting the Anglo-Saxon type of John
Bull. Instead, they usually portray him as a sort of sad-
faced travesty upon Lord Dundreary, a tall, lank, much
bewhiskered " milord," familiar to patrons of Continental
farce-comedy. But it is not in cases like these that race
prejudice becomes interesting. There is nothing subtle or

suggestive in mere vituperation, whether verbal or pictorial, any more than in the persistent representation of a nation by a type which is no sense representative. On the other hand, the subtle variations of expression in the John Bull of contemporary American artists, or the Uncle Sam of British caricature, will repay careful study. They form a sort of sensitive barometer of public sentiment in the two countries, and excepting during the rare periods of exceptional good feeling there is always in the Englishman's conception of Uncle Sam a scarce-concealed suggestion of crafty malice in place of his customary kindly shrewdness, while conversely, our portrayal of John Bull is only too apt to convert that bluff, honest-hearted country gentleman into a sort of arrogant blusterer, greedy for gain, yet showing the vein of cowardice distinctive of the born bully.

CHAPTER XXIX

YEARS OF TURBULENCE

IN marked contrast to the preceding lengthy period of tranquillity, the closing decade of the nineteenth century witnessed a succession of wars and international crises well calculated to stimulate the pencils of every cartoonist worthy of the name. One has only to recall that to this period belong the conflict between China and Japan, the brief clash between Greece and Turkey, the beginning of our policy of expansion, with the annexation of Hawaii, our own war with Spain, and England's protracted struggle in the Transvaal, to realize how rich in stirring events these few years have been, and what opportunities they offer for dramatic caricature.

A cartoon produced in an earlier chapter, entitled "Waiting," showed General Gordon gazing anxiously across the desert at the mirage which was conjured up by his fevered brain, taking the clouds of the horizon to be the guns of the approaching British army of relief. Early in 1885 the relief expedition started under the command of General Henry Stewart, and on February 7 there was published in *Punch* the famous cartoon "At Last," showing the meeting between Gordon and the relieving general. This was a famous *Punch* slip. That meeting never occurred. For on February 5, two days before the appearance of the issue containing the cartoon, Khartoum had been taken by the Mahdi. The following week Tenniel followed up "At Last" with the cartoon "Too Late," which

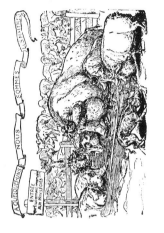

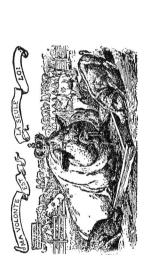

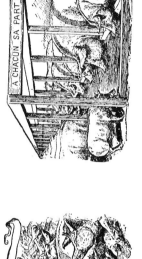

I. ABSOLUTE MONARCHY. II. CONSTITUTIONAL GOVERNMENT.

III. MIDDLE CLASS REPUBLIC. IV. SOCIAL REPUBLIC.

A PRESENT DAY LESSON.

From the "Revue Encyclopédique."

AT LAST!

A *Punch* slip : a cartoon published in anticipation of an event which did *not* occur—viz., the meeting of General Gordon and General Stewart at Khartoum.

By Tenniel, February 7, 1885.

"TOO LATE!"

*Telegram, Thursday Morning, Feb. 5.—"*Khartoum taken by the Mahdi. General Gordon's fate uncertain."

By Tenniel, February 14, 1885.

THE CHALLENGE.

PENANCE!

"HIS HONOUR ROOTED IN DISHONOUR STOOD, AND FAITH UNFAITHFUL MADE HIM FALSELY TRUE." TENNYSON.

THE LONDON "TIMES" AND THE SPURIOUS PARNELL LETTERS.

DROPPING THE PILOT.

TENNIEL'S FAMOUS CARTOON AT THE TIME OF
BISMARCK'S RETIREMENT.

showed the Mahdi and his fanatic following pouring into
Khartoum, while stricken Britannia covers her eyes.

The *Times* challenge to Charles Stewart Parnell was, of
course, recorded in the caricature of *Punch*. The "Thun-
derer," it will be remembered, published letters, which it
believed to be genuine, involving Parnell in the murders of
Lord Frederick Cavendish and Mr. Burke in Phœnix Park,
Dublin, in 1882. When these letters were proved to have
been forged by Pigot, *Punch* published a cartoon showing

the *Times* doing penance. Both of these cartoons were by
Tenniel. " The Challenge " appeared in the issue of April
30, 1887, and " Penance " almost two years later, March
9, 1889.

A cartoon which marked Tenniel's genius at its height, a
cartoon worthy of being ranked with that which depicted
the British Lion's vengeance on the Bengal Tiger after the
atrocities of the Sepoy rebellion, was his famous " Dropping
the Pilot," which was published on March 29, 1890, after
William II. of Germany had decided to dispense with the
services of the Iron Chancellor. Over the side of the ship

L'ENFANT TERRIBLE.
The Baccarat Scandal at Tranby Croft in 1891.
From " Puck."

of state the young Emperor is leaning complacently looking down on the grim old pilot, who has descended the ladder and is about to step into the boat that is to bear him ashore. The original sketch of this cartoon was finished by Tenniel as a

WILLIAM BLUEBEARD.
" My first two wives are dead. Take care, Hohenlohe, lest the same fate overtake you."
From " La Silhouette " (Paris).

commission from Lord Rosebery, who gave it to Bismarck. The picture is said to have pleased both the Emperor and the Prince.

The baccarat scandal at Tranby Croft and the subsequent trial at which the then Prince of Wales was present as a witness was a rich morsel for the caricaturist in the early summer of 1891. Not only in England, but on the Continent and in this country, the press was full of jibes and banter at the Prince's expense. The German comic paper,

Ulk, suggested pictorially a new coat-of-arms for his Royal Highness in which various playing cards, dice, and chips were much in evidence.   In another issue the same paper gives a German reading from Shakspere in which it censures the Prince in much the same manner that Falstaff censured the wild Harry of Henry IV.   The London cartoonists all had their slings with varying good nature.   *Fun* represented the Prince as the Prodigal Son being forgiven by the paternal British nation.   Point to this cartoon was given by the fact that the pantomime " L'Enfant Prodigue " was being played at the time in the Prince of Wales' Theater.   The *Pall Mall Budget* showed the Queen and the Heir Apparent enjoying a quiet evening over the card table at home.   The Prince is saying: " Ah, well! I must give up baccarat and take to cribbage with mamma."

Moonshine, in a cartoon entitled " Aren't they Rather

CHRISTIANITY AND THE BIBLE IN CHINA.
An exact copy of a Chinese native cartoon.   Reproduced in the San Francisco " Wasp," Jan. 2, 1892.

Overdoing it?" took a kindlier and a more charitable view of the whole affair. His Royal Highness is explaining the matter to a most horrible looking British Pharisee. "Don't be too hard on me, Mr. Stiggins," he says. "I am not such a bad sort of a fellow, on the whole. You mustn't believe all that you read in the papers." The nature of the American

JAPAN—"DOES IT HURT UP THERE?"
From "Kladderadatsch."

caricature of the scandal may be understood from the cartoon which we reproduce from *Puck*. This cartoon speaks for itself.

The Emperor William and his chancellors inspired *La Silhouette*, of Paris, to a very felicitous cartoon entitled "William Bluebeard." William is warning Hohenlohe and

BUSINESS AT THE DEATH-BED—UNCLE SAM AS UNDERTAKER.

From "Kladderadatsch" (Berlin).

THE START FOR THE CHINA CUP.

From "Moonshine" (London).

pointing to a closet in which are hanging the bodies of Bismarck and Caprivi, robed in feminine apparel. "My first two wives are dead," says Bluebeard. "Take care, Hohenlohe, lest the same fate overtake you!"

The increase in European armament in 1892 suggested to Tenniel the idea of the cartoon "The Road to Ruin," which appeared November 5 of that year. It shows the figures of two armed horsemen, France and Germany, each burdened with armies of four million men, riding along "The Road to Ruin." Their steeds, weighed down by the burdens

TABLEAU.
End of the Chinese-Japanese War.
From Toronto "Grip."

they bear, are faltering in their strides. A cartoon published shortly afterwards in the London *Fun* shows the figure of Peace welcoming the emperors of Germany and Austria, and urging them hospitably to lay aside their sword-belts. "Thanks, Madam," rejoins Kaiser Wilhelm, "but we would rather retain them—in your behalf!"

The brief war between China and Japan was necessarily of a nature to suggest cartoons of infinite variety. It was the quick, aggressive bantam against a huge but unwieldy opponent, and one of the earliest cartoons in *Punch* utilized

this idea in " The Corean Cock Fight." The big and clumsy
Shanghai is warily watching his diminutive foe, while the
Russian bear, contentedly squatting in the background, is
saying softly to himself: " Hi! whichever wins, I see my way
to a dinner." Every feature of Chinese life offered something to the caricaturists. For instance, in a cartoon entitled
" The First Installment," London *Fun* shows the Jap slashing
off the Chinaman's pigtail. Now this idea of the pigtail in one
form or another was carried through to the end of the war.
For example the Berlin *Ulk* offers a simple solution of the
whole controversy in a picture entitled " How the Northern
Alexander Might Cut the Corean Knot." China and Japan,
with their pigtails hopelessly tangled in a knot labeled
" Corea," are tugging desperately in opposite directions,
while Russia, knife in one hand and scissors in the other, is
preparing to cut off both pigtails close to the heads of his two
victims.

Punch characteristically represented the contending nations

THE CHINESE EXCLUSION ACT.
From the San Francisco " Wasp."

THE GREAT REPUBLICAN CIRCUS.

This is considered by Mr. Opper as one of his most effective political cartoons.

as two boys engaged in a street fight, while the various powers of Europe are looking on. John Chinaman has obviously had very much the worst of the fray; his features are battered; he is on the ground, and bawling lustily, " Boohoo! he hurtee me welly much! No peacey man come stoppy him! " The end of the war was commemorated by Toronto

TO THE RESCUE !

Grip in a tableau showing a huge Chinaman on his knees, while a little Jap is standing on top of the Chinaman's head toying with the defeated man's pigtail. *Kladderadatsch,* of Berlin, printed a very amusing and characteristic cartoon when the war was at an end: " Business at the death-bed— Uncle Sam as Undertaker." This pictorial skit alludes to the proposition from the United States that China pay her

A PILGRIM'S PROGRESS.

Mr. Gladstone in the Valley.

war indemnity to Japan in silver. It shows a stricken Chinaman tucked in a ludicrous bed and about to breathe his last. Uncle Sam, as an enterprising undertaker, has thrust his way in and insists on showing the dying man his handsome new style of coffin.

Still another clever cartoon in which the *Kladderadatsch* summed up the situation at the close of the war shows a map

THE BOULANGER EXCITEMENT.
The Noisy Boy in the European Lodging House.
From "Judge."

"YES, CITIZENS, SINCE THE DISARMAMENT THIS HAS BEEN MADE INTO A TELESCOPE. FORTUNATELY
IT WAS NOT A MUZZLE-LOADER, SO THEY HAVE BEEN ABLE TO PUT IN A LENS AT BOTH ENDS."

A French cartoon aimed at the Peace Conference.

of the eastern hemisphere, distorted into a likeness of a much-perturbed lady, the British Isles forming her coiffure, Europe her arms and body, and Asia the flowing drapery of her skirts.   Japan, saw in hand, has just completed the amputation of one of her feet—Formosa—and has the other—Corea—half sawn off.   " Does it hurt you up there? " he is asking, gazing up at the European portion of his victim. The same periodical a few months later forcibly called attention to the fact that while France and Russia were both profiting by the outcome of the war, Germany was likely to go away empty-handed.   It is entitled " The Partition of the Earth; an Epilogue to the Chinese Loan."   China, represented as a fat, overgrown mandarin, squatting comfortably on his throne, serene in the consciousness that his

A FIXTURE.

financial difficulties are adjusted for the time being, is explaining the situation to Prince Hohenlohe, who is waiting, basket in hand, for a share of the spoils.   On one side Russia is bearing off a toy engine and train of cars, labeled " Manchuria," and on the other France is contentedly jingling the keys to a number of Chinese seaports.   " The world has been given away," China is saying; " Kwangtung, Kwangsi,

A GROUP OF MODERN FRENCH CARICATURISTS.

and Yünnan are no longer mine. But if you will live in my celestial kingdom you need not feel any embarrassment; your uselessness has charmed us immensely."

The Boulanger excitement, which so roused France until the bubble was effectually pricked by the lawyer Floquet's fencing sword, was satirized by *Judge* in a cartoon entitled "The Noisy Boy in the European Lodging House." The scene is a huge dormitory in which the various European powers have just settled down in their separate beds for a quiet night's rest when Boulanger, with a paper cap on his head, comes marching through, loudly beating a drum. In an instant all is turmoil. King Humbert of Italy is shown in the act of hurling his royal boot at the offending intruder. The Czar of Russia has opened his eyes and his features are distorted with wrath. Bismarck is shaking his iron fist. The Emperor of Austria is getting out of bed, apparently with the intention of inflicting dire punishment on the interrupter of his slumbers. Even the Sultan of Turkey, long accustomed to disturbances from all quarters, has joined in the popular outcry. The lodgers with one voice are shouting, "Drat that Boy! Why doesn't he let us have some rest?"

The old allegorical ideal of Christian passing through the dangers of the Valley of the Shadow of Death in Bunyan's "Pilgrim's Progress," which has been appearing in caricature every now and then since Gillray used it against Napoleon, was employed by Tenniel in a cartoon of Mr. Gladstone and Home Rule published in *Punch*, April 15, 1893. The old warrior, sword in hand, is making his way slowly along the narrow and perilous wall of Home Rule. On either side are the bogs of disaster, suggestive of his fate in case his foot should slip.

The Panama scandals in France and the ensuing revela-

tions of general political trickery suggested one of Sambourne's best cartoons, that depicting France descending into
the maelstrom of corruption.   This cartoon appeared in the

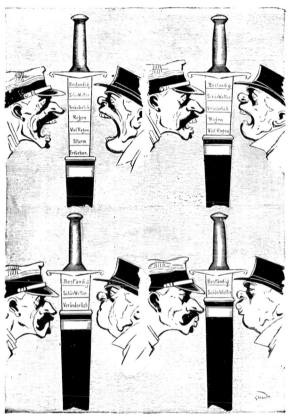

THE ANGLO-FRENCH WAR BAROMETER.
FASHODA !!! FASHODA !! Fashoda ! Fashoda.
From " Kladderadatsch " (Berlin).

beginning of 1893.   It shows France in the figure of a
woman going supinely over the rapids, to be hurled into the
whirlpool below.

British feeling on the Fashoda affair was summed up by
Tenniel in two cartoons which appeared in October and
November, in 1898.   The first of these called " Quit—Pro

Quo?" was marked by a vindictive bitterness which appeared rather out of place in the *Punch* of the last quarter of the century.   But it must be remembered that for a brief time feeling ran very high in both countries over the affair.   In this cartoon France is represented as an organ-grinder who persists in grinding out the obnoxious Fashoda tune to the intense annoyance of the British householder. The second cartoon represents the Sphinx with the head of John Bull.   John Bull is grimly winking his left eye, to signify that he regards himself very much of a " fixture " in Egypt.

CHAPTER XXX

AMERICAN PARTIES AND PLATFORMS

THE dangerous condition in which the United States found itself about the time we began the building of our new and greater navy was depicted in *Judge* by the cartoon entitled, " Rip Van Winkle Awakes at Last." It shows a white-bearded, white-haired Uncle Sam seated on a rock about which the tide is rapidly rising, looking round at the great modern armaments of England and France and Germany and Italy, and murmuring, as he thinks of his own antiquated wooden ships of war and brick forts, " Why, I'm twenty years behind the age." In his old hat, with the broken crown, are the feathers of Farragut, Perry, Paul Jones, and Lawrence, but these alone are not enough, nor will even the " Spirit of '76," which hovers over him in the shape of an eagle, quite suffice. He has his musket of 1812 and his muzzle-loading gun of 1864, but in the background are those huge cannon of European foes and above them is the gaunt, grim figure of a helmeted Death. A little more and it would have been too late. Now there is yet time. Rip Van Winkle awakes at last.

An interesting variant upon the old type of " Presidential Steeplechase " cartoons appeared in *Puck* during the summer of 1892, after the Republican convention at Minneapolis and the Democratic convention at Chicago had respectively nominated Mr. Harrison and Mr. Cleveland. The cartoon is entitled " They're Off ! " and is drawn with admirable spirit. The scene is a Roman amphitheater, and the two

Presidential candidates, in the guise of charioteers, are guiding their mettlesome steeds in a mad gallop around the arena. Mr. Cleveland's horses, " Tariff Reform " and " Economy," are running steadily, and seem to be slowly forging to the front, while those of Mr. Harrison, " High Protection " and

RIP VAN WINKLE AWAKES AT LAST.
By Gillam in "Judge."

" Force Bill," are not pulling well together, and with ears pointed forward, look as though they might at any moment become unmanageable.

In connection with this campaign of 1892, there was no cartoon of more interest than that entitled " Where Am I At? " which Bernard Gillam drew for *Judge*, and this in-

THEY'RE OFF!
The Presidential race between Harrison and Cleveland in 1892.
From " Puck."

terest lies less in the cartoon itself than in the amusing story of its conception and execution. Right up to election day not only Gillam, but the entire staff of *Judge*, were perfectly confident of Republican success at the polls. To them the election seemed to be a mere formality which had to be gone through with, in order that General Harrison might remain in the White House for four years more. So a conference was held, after which Mr. Gillam began work on the cartoon which was to commemorate the Republican victory. The idea used was that of a general smash-up, with Mr. Cleveland in the middle of the *débâcle* and the Republican elephant marching triumphantly over the ruins. Along these lines a double-page cartoon was drawn with an immense variety of detail, reproduced, and made ready for the press. Election Day came around, and a few hours after the polls had been closed it became evident, to the consternation of Mr. Gillam and his associates, that instead of the expected Republican victory, Mr. Cleveland had swept the country by overwhelm-

"WHERE AM I AT?"

The famous redrawn cartoon which in its original form depicted Mr. Cleveland and the
Democratic Party disastrously routed at the polls in 1892.

By Gillam in "Judge."

ing majorities.   What was to be done?   It was too late to prepare another cartoon, so that the plate already made was taken from the press, and the cartoonist set to work.   To the discomfited countenance of Mr. Cleveland Gillam attached a beard which transformed the face into a likeness to that of the defeated Republican candidate.   A huge patch drawn over one of the eyes of the Republican elephant changed its appearance of elation to one of the most woebegone depression.   Other slight changes in the legends here and there throughout the picture transformed its nature to such an extent that only the most practiced eye could detect anything that was not wholly spontaneous and genuine.   To cap it all, in a corner of the picture Gillam drew a likeness of himself in the form of a monkey turning an uncomfortable somersault.   With a knowledge of these facts the reader by a close examination of this cartoon, which is reproduced in this volume, will undoubtedly detect the lines along which the lightning change was made.   Nevertheless, it will be impossible for him to deny that the transformation was cleverly done.

Besides being the year of the Presidential campaign, 1892 was a year when the thoughts of Americans were turned backward four centuries to the time when Christopher Columbus first landed on the shore of the Western Hemisphere.   The original ships of Columbus's fleet were being brought over the water from Spain; the Columbus idea was being exploited everywhere in topical song and light opera; and it would have been strange indeed if it had failed to play some part in political caricature.   Gillam in *Judge* made use of it in the cartoon entitled " The Political Columbus Who Will NOT Land in '92."   It represents the ship of the Democracy with Mr. Cleveland as Columbus gazing anxiously and uneasily

THE POLITICAL COLUMBUS WHO WILL NOT LAND IN 1892.

By Gillam in "Judge."

at the horizon.   At the bow of the ship is the lion's head and the shield of Britannia, in allusion to Mr. Cleveland's alleged pro-English sympathies.   The sail upon which the ship is relying for its progress is marked " Free Trade " and is a woefully patched and weather-beaten bit of canvas.   The crew of the ship is a strange assortment which suggests all sorts of mutiny and piracy.   In the front of the vessel and close behind the captain are Dana, Croker, Sheehan, and Hill.   Beyond them we see the figures of Cochran, Carlisle,

Crisp, Brice, and Mills and Flower.   In the far aft are Blackburn and Gorman.   Evidently crew and captain are animated by despair, although the gull, bearing the features of Mr. Pulitzer, of the New York *World,* that is circling around the ship, shows that land is not so many miles away. " I don't see land," cries Cleveland-Columbus.   And the despairing crew, pointing to the Free Trade sail, calls back, " And you never will with that rotten canvas."

In contrast with the vindictive and malicious character of

the cartoons which heralded Mr. Cleveland's first election, there was a marked absence of unpleasant personalities in those which belong to the period of his second term. There was no disposition, however, to spare him in regard to the growing difficulty he had in holding his party together or his assumption of what Republicans regarded as an entirely unwarranted degree of authority. This autocratic spirit was cleverly satirized by a cartoon in *Judge*, to which allusion has already been made. It consists simply of a map of the United States so drawn as to form a grotesque likeness of the President. He is bending low in an elaborate bow, in which mock-humility and glowing self-satisfaction are amusingly blended, his folded hands forming the Florida peninsula, his coat-tails projecting into lower California. Beneath is inscribed the following paraphrase:

> My country, 'tis of ME,
> Sweet land of liberty,
> Of ME I sing!

Mr. Cleveland's troubles with his party began early in his second administration. As early as April we find him depicted by *Judge* as the "Political Bull in the Democratic China-Shop." The bull has already had time to do a vast amount of havoc. The plate-glass window, commanding a view of the national capitol, is a wreck, and the floor is strewn with the remains of delicate cups and platters, amidst which may still be recognized fragments of the "Baltimore Machine," "Rewards for Workers," "Wishes of the Leaders," etc. An elaborate vase, marked "N. Y. Machine," and bearing a portrait of Senator Hill, is just toppling over, to add its fragments to the general wreckage.

The general depression of trade and the much-debated issue of tariff reform recur again and again in the caricatures

RETURN OF THE SOUTHERN FLAGS.
By Gillam in "Judge."

of the second Cleveland administration, especially after the Republican landslide of 1893. Thus, in December of that year, a significant cartoon in *Judge* represents the leading statesmen of each party engaged in a game of "National Football," the two goals being respectively marked "Protection" and "Free Trade." "Halfback" Hill is saying, "Brace up, Cap; we've got the ball," and Captain Grover, nursing a black eye, rejoins disconsolately, "That's all very well, boys, but they've scored against us, and we've got to put up the game of our lives to beat them." In January the same periodical published a pessimistic sketch, showing Uncle Sam, shivering with cold, and his hands plunged deep into his pockets, gloomily watching the mercury in the "Industrial Thermometer" sinking steadily lower from protection and plenty, through idleness, misery, and starvation, to the zero point of free trade. "Durn the Democratic weather, anyway," says Uncle Sam. A more hopeful view of the situation found expression in *Puck,* in a cartoon entitled "Relief at Hand." Labor, in the guise of an Alpine traveler, has fallen by the wayside, and lies half buried beneath the snows of the "McKinley Tariff." Help, however, has come, in the form of a St. Bernard, named "Wilson Tariff Bill," while Cleveland, in the guise of a monk, is hastening from the neighboring monastery, drawn in the semblance of the national capitol. Still another cartoon harping on the need of tariff reform represents McKinley and the other leading Republicans as "Ponce de Leon and His Followers," gathered around a pool labeled "High Protection Doctrine." "They think it is the fountain of political youth and strength, but it is only a stagnant pool that is almost dried up." Among the many caricatures in which *Judge* supported the opposite side, and heaped ridicule on

THE CHAMPION MASHER OF THE UNIVERSE.

By *Gillam in "Judge."*

the Wilson Bill, one of the best shows Uncle Sam retiring
for the night, and examining with disgust and wrath the
meager crazy quilt (the Wilson Bill) with which he has been

THE HARRISON PLATFORM.
By Keppler in " Puck."

provided in lieu of blankets. " I'll freeze to death," he is
grumbling, " and yet some of those idiots call this a protec-
tive measure."

Mr. Cleveland's determination to return to the South the
flags captured in the War of Secession, in the hopes of put-
ting an end to sectional feeling, brought down upon his head
the wrath of the more extreme Republican element, a wrath

which was reflected strongly, editorially and pictorially, in the
papers of the day. This suggested to *Judge* the cartoon entitled " Halt," in which Mr. Cleveland, in the act of handing
back the captured flags, is restrained by the spirit of Lincoln,
which says, " Had you fought for those flags you would not
be so quick to give them away!" To which Mr. Cleveland
is made to reply, " Great Scott! I thought you were dead and
forgotten long ago. I only meant to please Mr. Solid South.
They're rubbish, anyhow." This is another cartoon from
the hand of the prolific Gillam.

The movement for the annexation of the Hawaiian
Islands, which occurred in the spring of 1893, and which
many Americans were inclined to regard with suspicion and
disfavor, was commemorated in a great variety of cartoons,
both in this country and abroad. It was only natural that a
movement which owed its inception to a Republican administration, should receive the cordial approval and indorse-
ment of *Judge*. A cartoon, dated February 18, represents
Columbia in the guise of an exemplary modern school-mis-
tress, serenely holding in order her turbulent class of mingled
Chinese, negroes, Indians, Italian organ-grinders, and Russian anarchists, while she gives a cordial welcome to the
small, half-naked new scholar from the Pacific, who is timidly
begging to be admitted. Canada, represented as a demure
little maiden, stands just behind Hawaii, an interested spectator, apparently more than half inclined to follow his example.
In much the same spirit was a design that appeared in the
Wasp, representing Uncle Sam in the character of St. Peter,
holding the key to America's political paradise. " Poor
little imp," he is saying to the Hawaiian applicant, " I don't
see why I should shut you out, when I've let in all the tramps
of the world already." Another cartoon which appeared in

THE END OF THE CHILIAN AFFAIR.
From "Judge."

Judge was entitled, "The Champion Masher of the Universe." This represents Hawaii under the form of a dusky but comely damsel, being borne off complacently by a gorgeously attired Uncle Sam, while his discomfited rivals are looking on in chagrin and disgust. These rivals are England, under the form of John Bull; France, shown under the features of President Sadi Carnot; Germany, the Emperor William; and Italy, King Humbert. This cartoon was drawn by Gillam.

The Toronto *Grip* saw the matter in quite a different aspect. Hawaii, a badly frightened savage, is bound to a stake, while Uncle Sam, in the guise of a missionary, is whetting the knife of annexation, preparing to give him the *coup-de-grace,* and at the same time waving off John Bull, who holds his knife, "Protectorate," with similar intent. "Hold up," says Hawaii, "didn't you say it was wrong to eat man?" and Uncle Sam rejoins benevolently, "Yes—

but—well, circumstances alter cases, and the interests of civilization and commerce, you know—— You keep off, John; he's my meat." The suggestion that England was merely waiting for a good excuse to step in and take possession of Hawaii, while the American administration and Congress were trying to reach an understanding, was eagerly seized upon by other journals as well as *Grip,* especially in Germany. The Berlin *Ulk* portrayed Queen Liliuokalani, armed with a broom, angrily sweeping Uncle Sam from his foothold in Honolulu, while John Bull, firmly established on two of the smaller islands, " laughs to his heart's content," so the legend runs, " but the Yankee is mad with rage." In similar spirit the *Kladderadatsch* depicts John Bull and Uncle Sam as " Two Good Old Friends," trying to " balance their interests in the Pacific Ocean." With clasped hands the two rivals are see-sawing backwards and forwards, each striving to retain a precarious foothold, as they straddle the Pacific from Samoa to Hawaii, and each quite oblivious of the discomfort of the squirming little natives that they are crushing under heel.

The fiasco of Mr. Cleveland's attempt to restore Queen Liliuokalani to her throne was hit off in *Judge* by a cartoon portraying him as Don Quixote, physically much the worse for wear, as a result of his latest tilt at the Hawaiian windmill. The knight's spirit, however, is unbroken, and he is receiving philosophically the well-meant consolation of Sancho Panza Gresham.

Another cartoon of sterling literary flavor is that representing Mr. McKinley as a political Tam o' Shanter, which appeared during the exciting election of 1896. The countenance of Tam in this cartoon shows none of the anxiety and mental perturbation of the hero of Burns' poems. You

MR. McKINLEY AS A POLITICAL TAM O'SHANTER.

By Gillam in "Judge."

DON QUIXOTE BRYAN MEETS DISASTER IN HIS ENCOUNTER WITH
THE FULL DINNER PAIL.
By Victor Gillam in "Judge."

can see that he has full confidence in his good mare, " National Credit," and is perfectly convinced that she will carry
him unscathed over the road to Good Times, Prosperity, and
Protection. The carlins have been close at his mare's heels,
however, and as he passes the bridge over which they dare

OUTING OF THE ANARCHISTS.

not cross, the foremost of his pursuers has caught and pulled away as a trophy the tail of the steed. The tail, however, is something with which he can well part, for it typifies four years of business depression. The leaders of the pursuing carlins are Free Trade, Anarchy, Sectionalism, and Popocracy.

Mr. Bryan's appeal to the farmer in 1896 was hit off by Hamilton in a powerful, but exceedingly blasphemous, car-

TO THE DEATH.

toon entitled " The Temptation." Bryan in the form of a huge angel of darkness has taken the farmer to the top of a high mountain to show him the riches of the world. As far as the eye can see stretch oceans and cities and hills and rivers and mountains of silver. It is a great pity that so grim and powerful a cartoon should have been marred by that display of bad taste which has been too frequent in the history of caricature.

The caricature produced by the campaign between Mr. McKinley and Mr. Bryan in 1900 offers few, if any, cartoons more admirable than that by Mr. Victor Gillam, representing

Don Quixote Bryan meeting disaster in his fight against the full dinner pail. This cartoon has that literary flavor which has been too much lacking in American caricature, and which raises this particular cartoon far above the average in the same school. The idea, of course, is based on Don Quixote's disastrous encounter with the windmill, which that poor crack-brained gentleman took to be a giant. The body of the windmill is a huge dinner pail and its arms are a crossed knife and fork. Don Quixote, incased in armor from head to foot, and mounted on the Democratic donkey with free silver for a saddle, has tilted against the solid structure with disastrous results. His lance is shattered, and he and his

" WE ARE THE PEOPLE."

faithful steed lie prostrate and discomfited on opposite sides of the road. The Sancho Panza needed to complete the picture appears under the familiar features of Mr. Richard Croker, who, leading the Tammany Tiger by a rope, is hurrying to his master's assistance. In the distance may be seen the White House, but the road in that direction is completely barred by the stanch windmill that has so successfully resisted the mad knight's onslaught.

CHAPTER XXXI

THE SPANISH-AMERICAN WAR

THE pent-up feeling throughout the United States, which reached a dangerous degree of tension during the weeks preceding the declaration of war against Spain, was forcibly symbolized in the Minneapolis *Herald*. The dome of the National Capitol is portrayed, surmounted by a " Congressional safety-valve." McKinley, clinging to the cupola, is anxiously listening to the roar of the imprisoned steam, which is escaping in vast " war clouds," in spite of all the efforts of Speaker Reed, who is freely perspiring in his effort to hold down the valve.

One of those cartoons which are not to be forgotten in a day or a week or a month; one which stirs the blood and rouses the mind to a new patriotism even when seen years after the events which inspired it, is Victor Gillam's " Be Careful! It's Loaded!" which appeared a few weeks before the outbreak of the Spanish-American War and which we deem worthy of being ranked among the twenty-five or thirty great cartoons which the nineteenth century has produced. To realize to-day its full force and meaning one has to recall the peculiar tension under which the American people were laboring during the months of February, March, and April, 1898. The *Maine* had been destroyed in Havana Harbor, and although, now that anger has died down, we can no longer cling implacably to the belief, which was then everywhere expressed, that it was an act emanating from the Spanish Government, at the time it was too much for our over-

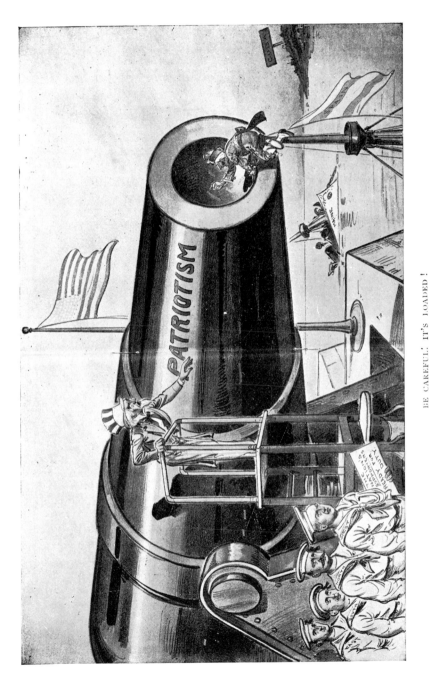

BE CAREFUL! IT'S LOADED!

By *Victor Gillam in "Judge."*

wrought nerves; the condition of Cuba was growing every day more deplorable, and everyone felt that the inevitable conflict was hourly at hand.   In the picture American patriotism is symbolized by a huge cannon.   A diminutive Spaniard has climbed to the top of a mast of a Spanish vessel and monkey-like is shaking his fist down the muzzle.   Uncle Sam, standing by the gun and realizing the Spaniard's im-

Speaker Reed to McKinley—"You've got to bank the fire some way or other: I can't hold in this steam much longer."

Minneapolis "Tribune."

minent peril calls out, excitedly, " Be Careful!   It's Loaded! " a warning to which the latter seems little inclined to pay any attention.   In its very simplicity this cartoon differs greatly from most of those of the school of *Puck* and *Judge*.   There is none of that infinite variety of detail which makes an elaborate study necessary in order to arrive at a full comprehension of the meaning of a cartoon.   " Be careful! It's Loaded! " like the most striking English and French cartoons, may be understood at a glance.

A cartoon like Grant E. Hamilton's "The Latest War
Bulletin" we find amusing at the present time.   We did not

THE LATEST WAR BULLETIN.
By Hamilton in "Judge."

find it so a little over five years ago.   This latest war bulletin,
printed in asbestos, is supposed to have been just received
from the infernal regions.   His Satanic majesty, with a sar-
donic grin upon his face, has just composed it to his own
entire satisfaction.   Marked up on the burning furnace of
Hades it reads: "Only Spanish will be spoken here until
further notice—P. S.   Guests will please leave their crowns
and Spanish 4's in charge of the night clerk."

Another equally hideous cartoon by Hamilton is that
entitled "The Spanish Brute Adds Mutilation to Murder."
It shows a hideous ape-like monster representing Spain, one
blood-dripping hand smearing the tombstones erected to the
sailors of the *Maine* and the other clutching a reeking knife.
All about him under the tropical trees are the bodies of his

A knife for the American pigs.

PIRATICAL—(Spain accused an American ship of flying the Spanish flag in order to cut the cable.)

The result of the war—defeats.

SAMPSON—"Where is Cervera's fleet?"

McKinley and England.

McKINLEY—"I wonder what he holds?"

The Minister of Revenue has a spoon for the war kettle.

SPANISH CARTOONS OF THE SPANISH-AMERICAN WAR.

From "Don Quijote" (Madrid).

mutilated victims. The expression of the monster's countenance is a lesson in national prejudice. It shows how far a
well-balanced nation may go in moments of bitterness and
anger.

One of the most striking and amusing of all the cartoons
evoked by the results of the Spanish-American War appeared in *Punch* at a time when our departure from our

THE SPANISH BRUTE—ADDS MUTILATION TO MURDER.
By Hamilton in "Judge."

traditional policy began to cause comment in Europe. There
are two figures, that of Dame Europa and that of Uncle Sam.
Dame Europa is a lady of frigid aspect, with arms folded,
and who has drawn herself up to full height as she gazes
scornfully at the complacent and unruffled Uncle Sam. " To
whom do I owe the honor of this intrusion? " she asks icily.
" Marm, my name is Uncle Sam." " Any relation of the
late Colonel Monroe? " is the scathing retort.

No less interesting than the American cartoons of the Spanish War are those contributed by Spain herself, although in the light of subsequent events they are chiefly amusing for their overweening confidence and braggadocio insolence. Among the more extravagant flights of Spanish imagination, which later news turned into absurdities, may be cited " Dewey's Situation," in which the victor of Manila is represented as a disconsolate rat, caught in the Philippine mouse-trap; " Cervera bottles up Schley," a situation which the sober facts of history afterwards reversed; and " McKinley's Condition," in which the President is represented as swathed in bandages, and suffering severely from apocryphal injuries received at Porto Rico and Cienfuegos. All of these cartoons appeared at different times in the Madrid *Don Quijote,* which did not always keep on this level of empty boasting, but occasionally produced some really clever caricature. A regular feature of the Spanish War cartoons was the American Hog as a symbol of the United States, and some of the applications of this idea in the *Don Quijote* were distinctly amusing. For instance, in reference to Spain's accusation that an American ship flew the Spanish flag at Guantanamo in order to approach near enough to cut the cable, America is shown as a fat hog, triumphantly strutting along on its hind legs and ostentatiously waving the Spanish colors. Again, the Sampson-Schley controversy is hit off in a picture showing Sampson surrounded by a number of naval " hogs," each armed with gigantic shears and bent upon obtaining the Admiral's scalp. Still another cartoon seeks to explain the " real purpose " in getting Cuba away from Spain. A drove of pigs have clustered around a huge barrel of Cuban molasses and are eagerly sucking the contents through tubes. Of a more dignified type are the caricatures

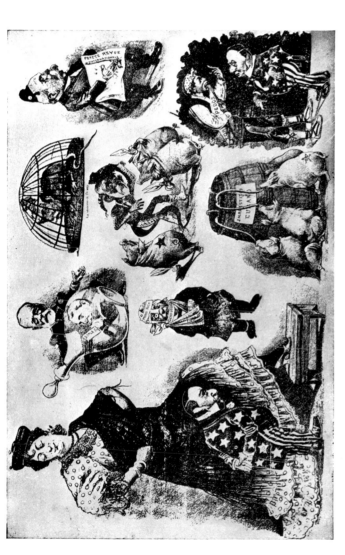

"You can't unbuckle that shoe."

Cervera bottles up Schley.
McKinley's condition.

Dewey's situation.
After Sampson's scalp.
America's Real Desire.

Castelar writes a letter.
"This is for you if you don't behave."

SPANISH CARTOONS OF THE SPANISH-AMERICAN WAR.

From the "Don Quijote" (Madrid).

representing Spain as a beautiful and haughty Señorita, boldly showing how she keeps beneath her garter " a knife for the American pigs "; or pointing to her shoe on which Cuba serves as a buckle, and arrogantly challenging a diminutive McKinley,—" you can't unbuckle that shoe! "

CHAPTER XXXII

THE BOER WAR AND THE DREYFUS CASE

A CARTOON which was a forerunner of the Transvaal War and the railway between Capetown and Cairo was that entitled "The Rhodes Colossus," which appeared in *Punch* December 10, 1892. It was by the hand of Linley Sambourne. It shows a colossal figure of Cecil

THE RHODES COLOSSUS
STRIDING FROM CAPE TOWN TO CAIRO.

By Linley Sambourne.

Rhodes standing on a map of Africa with one foot planted in Egypt and the other at the Cape. In his hands he holds a line suggesting the telegraph wire connecting the two places.

THE SITUATION IN SOUTH AFRICA.

By Gillam in "Judge."

Although the German Government refused to interfere in the protracted struggle in the Transvaal, the sympathy of Germany with the Boers found expression in a host of cartoons, bitterly inveighing against British aggression. Thoroughly characteristic is one which appeared in the *Lustige Blätter* entitled "English World-Kingdom; or, Bloody Cartography." A grossly distorted caricature of

THE ENGLISH WORLD KINGDOM, OR BLOODY
CARTOGRAPHY.
From the " Lustige Blätter."

Victoria is standing before a map of the world, and dipping her pen in a cup of blood, held for her by an army officer. Chamberlain, at her elbow, is explaining that " the lowest corner down yonder, must be painted red! " Another of the *Lustige Blätter's* grim cartoons, alluding to the terrible price in human life that England paid for her ultimate victory in the Transvaal, depicts Britannia, as Lady Macbeth,

vainly trying to wash the stain from her bloody hands.
"Out, damned spot!" In lighter vein is the cartoon which
is here reproduced from the *Wiener Humoristische Blätter*
showing "Oom Paul at His Favorite Sport." Kruger,

BRITANNIA AS LADY MACBETH TRYING TO WASH
AWAY THE STAINS OF THE BOER WAR.
From the "Lustige Blätter."

rakishly arrayed in tennis garb, is extracting infinite enjoy-
ment from the congenial exercise of volleying English
soldiers, dressed up as shuttlecocks, over the "Transvaal
net" into the watery ditch beyond.

Judged by the manner it was mirrored in the caricature of
Europe and America, the Dreyfus Case assumed the magnitude of a great war or a crisis in national existence. During
the last two or three years that the degraded Captain of
Artillery was a prisoner at Devil's Island, when Zola was
furiously accusing, and the General Staff was talking about

THE FLYING DUTCHMAN.

Minneapolis "Journal."

OOM PAUL'S FAVORITE PASTIME.
From the " Wiener Humoristische Blätter."

" the Honor of the Army," and France was divided into two
angry camps, one had only to glance at the current cartoons
to realize that Dreyfus was, as the late G. W. Steevens called
him, " the most famous man in the world." For a time the
great personages of the earth were relegated to the background. The monarchs and statesmen of Europe were of
interest and importance only so far as their careers affected
that of the formerly obscure Jewish officer.

Perhaps the most famous of all the admirable cartoons
dealing with *l'Affaire* was the " Design for a New French
Bastile," which was of German origin and which caused the
paper publishing it to be excluded from French territory. It
appeared just after Colonel Henry had cut his throat with a
razor in his cell in the Fortress of Vincennes, when suspicions
of collusion were openly expressed, and some went so far as
to hint that the prisoner's death might be a case of murder
and not suicide. The " Design for a New French Bastile "

UP AGAINST THE BREASTWORKS.

showed a formidable fortress on the lines of the famous prison destroyed in the French Revolution with a row of the special cells beneath. In one of these cells a loaded revolver was placed conspicuously on the chair; in the next was seen a sharpened razor; from a stout bar in a third cell dangled a convenient noose. The inference was obvious, and the fact that the cells were labeled " for Picquart," " for Zola,"

MR. RHODES—THE NAPOLEON OF SOUTH AFRICA.
From the Westminster " Budget" (London).

" for Labori " and the other defenders of Dreyfus gave the cartoon an added and sinister significance. In caricature the Dreyfus case was a battle between a small number of Anti-Dreyfussard artists on the one hand, and the Dreyfus press with all the cartoonists of Europe and the United States as its allies on the other. The opportunity to exalt the prisoner, to hold him up as a martyr, to interpret pictorially the spirit of Zola's ringing "*la verite est en marche, et rien ne l'arrê-tera!*" offered a vast field for dramatic caricature. On the other hand the cartoon against Dreyfus and his defenders was

FIRE !
From "Psst" (Paris).

essentially negative, and the wonder is that the rout of the minority was not greater—it should have been a veritable "*sauve qui peut.*"

The spirit of anti-Dreyfussard caricature was Anti-Semitism. One of the most striking of the cartoons on this

THE LAST PHASE OF THE DREYFUS CASE.
Justice takes Dreyfus into her car.
From "Amsterdammer."

side purported to contrast France before 1789 and France at the end of the Nineteenth Century. In the first picture we

TOWARD FREEDOM.

MADAME LA RÉPUBLIQUE—" Welcome, M. Le Capitaine. Let me hope that I may soon return you your
sword."

From " Punch " (London)

were shown a peasant toiling laboriously along a furrow in
the ground, bearing on his shoulders a beribboned and be-
plumed aristocrat of the old régime, whose thighs grip the
neck of the man below with the tenacity of the Old Man of
the Sea. That was France before the Revolution came with
its bloody lesson. In the picture showing France at the end
of the Nineteenth Century there was the same peasant toiling
along at the bottom, but the burden under which he tottered
was fivefold. Above him was the petty merchant, who in
turn carried on his shoulders the lawyer, and so on until riding along, arrogantly and ostentatiously, at the top was the
figure of the foreign-born Jew, secure through the possession of his tainted millions.

The dangerous straits through which the Waldeck-Rousseau ministry was obliged to pass were hit off in a cartoon appearing in the *Humoristische Blätter* of Berlin, entitled " Between Scylla and Charybdis." On one side of the narrow waterway a treacherous rock shows the yawning jaws of the Army. On the other side, equally hideous and threatening, gleam the sharpened teeth of the face typifying the

A DUTCH VIEW.
The present condition of the French general staff.
From " Amsterdammer."

Dreyfus Party. Waldeck-Rousseau, appreciating the choppiness of the sea and the dangerous rocks, calls to his gallant crew: " Forward, dear friends, look neither to the right nor to the left, and we will win through at last." Many of the cartoons dealing with the Dreyfus case were mainly symbolic in their nature; full of figures of " Justice with her Scales,"

" Justice Blindfolded and with Unsheathed Sword,"
" Swords of Damocles " and so on. A Dutch cartoon in
Amsterdammer, entitled " The Last Phase of the Dreyfus
Case," showed Justice taking the unfortunate captain into her
car. The horses drawing the car were led by Scheurer-
Kestner and Zola, while following the chariot, to which they
are linked by ignominious chains, were the discredited Chiefs
of the Army. The same paper humorously summed up the con-

BETWEEN SCYLLA AND CHARYBDIS.

WALDECK-ROUSSEAU—" Forward, dear friends,
look neither to the right nor the left, and we will
win through at last."

From " Humoristische Blätter " (Berlin).

dition of the French General Staff in a picture showing a falling house of which the occupants, pulling at cross-purposes,
were accelerating the downfall. The decision upon Revision
and the dispatching of the Spax to Cayenne to bring Dreyfus
back to France was commemorated in London *Punch* in a
dignified cartoon called " Toward Freedom." Madame la
République greeted Dreyfus: " Welcome, M. le Capitaine.

Let me hope I may soon return you your sword." The same phase of the case was more maliciously interpreted by *Lustige Blätter* of Berlin in a cartoon entitled "At Devil's Island," which showed the Master of the Island studying grinningly a number of officers whom he held in the hollow of his hand, and saying: "They take away one captain from me: but look here, a whole handful of generals! Oh, after all, the arrangement is not so bad."

AT DEVIL'S ISLAND.

THE MASTER OF THE ISLAND.—"They take away one captain from me; but look here, a whole handful of generals! Oh, after all, the arrangement is not so bad."

From "Lustige Blätter" (Berlin).

CHAPTER XXXIII

WITH the Spanish-American War, the *Affaire Dreyfus* in France, and England's long struggle for supremacy in the Transvaal, the period arbitrarily chosen as the scope of this book comes to a brilliant and dramatic close. But the cartoonist's work is never done. Nimble pencils are still busy, as in the days of Rowlandson and Gillray, in recording and in influencing the trend of history. And although, now and again during the past century, there has been some individual cartoonist whose work has stood out more boldly and prominently than the work of any one of our contemporaries in Europe or in this country stands out to-day, there has never been a time in the whole history of comic art when Caricature has held such sway and maintained such dignity, and has enlisted in her service so many workers of the first talent and rank. Without alluding to the men of France and England, what an array it is that contemporary American caricature presents! C. G. Bush of the New York *World,* Charles Nelan of the New York *Herald,* Frederick Burr Opper and Homer Davenport of the New York *American and Journal,* Mahoney of the Washington *Star,* Bradley of the Chicago *Evening News,* May of the Detroit *Journal,* " Bart " of the Minneapolis *Journal,* Mayfield of the New Orleans *Times-Democrat,* Victor Gillam, carrying on the traditions of his brother—Rogers, Walker, Hedrick, Bowman, McCutcheon, Lambdin, Wallace, Leipziger, Berryman, Holme, Barthole-

C. G. BUSH OF "THE WORLD." THE DEAN OF ACTIVE AMERICAN CARTOONISTS.

mew, Carter, Steele, Powers, Barritt—and to name these men does not nearly exhaust the list of those artists whose clever work has amused and unconsciously influenced hundreds of thousands of thinking American men and women.

There are interest and significance in the fact that a majority of the ablest caricaturists of to-day are devoting their talents almost exclusively to the daily press. It is an exacting sort of work, exhaustive both physically and mentally. The mere

WILLIE AND HIS PAPA.

"What on earth are you doing in there, Willie?"
'Teddy put me in. He says it's the best place for me during the campaign."

idea of producing a single daily cartoon, week in and week out,—thirty cartoons a month, three hundred and sixty-five cartoons a year, with the regularity of a machine,—is in itself appalling. And yet a steadily growing number of artists are turning to this class of work, and one reason for this is that they realize that through the medium of the daily press their influence is more far-reaching than it possibly can be in the pages of the comic weeklies, and that at the same time the exigencies of journalism allow more scope for individuality than do the carefully planned cartoons of papers like *Puck* or *Judge*. Speed and originality are the two prime requisites of the successful newspaper cartoon of to-day, a maximum of thought expressed in a minimum of lines, apposite, clear-cut, and incisive, like a well-written editorial. Indeed, our leading cartoonists regard their art as simply another and especially telling medium for giving expression to editorial opinion. Mr. Bush, "the dean of American caricaturists," may be said to have spoken for them all when he said, in a recent interview, that he looks upon a cartoon as an editorial pure and simple.

"To be a success it should point a moral. Exaggeration and a keen sense of humor are only adjuncts of the cartoonist, for he must deal with real people. He must also be a student. I am obliged not only to use my pencil, but to study hard, and read everything I can lay my hands on. The features of Roosevelt, Bryan, Hanna, and Croker may be familiar to me, but I must know what these men are doing. I must also know what the masses behind these popular characters think and believe."

Another direct result of the influence of journalism upon caricature, in addition to that of compelling the artist to keep in closer touch than ever before with contemporary history, is the growing popularity of the series method—a method which dates back to the Macaire of Philipon and the Mayeux of Travies, and which consists in portraying day by day the same more or less grotesque types, ever undergoing some new and absurd adventure. It is a method which suits the needs of artist and public alike. To the former, his growing familiarity with every line and detail of the features

HOMER DAVENPORT, OF THE "NEW YORK AMERICAN AND JOURNAL."

and forms of his pictorial puppets minimizes his daily task, while the public, even that part of the public which is opposed to comic art in general, or is out of sympathy with the political attitude of a certain series in particular, finds itself gradually becoming familiar with the series, through fugitive and unexpected glimpses, and ends by following the series with amusement and interest and a growing curiosity as to what new and absurd complications the artist will next introduce. This employment of the series idea is as successful in social as political satire. Mr. Outcault's "Yellow Kid" and "Buster Brown," Mr. Opper's "Happy Hooligan" and "Alphonse and Gaston," Gene Carr's "Lady Bountiful," and Carl Schultze's "Foxy Grandpa" are types that have won friends throughout the breadth of the continent. In the domain of strictly political caricature, however, there is no series that has attracted more attention than Homer Davenport's familiar conception of the Trusts, symbolized as a bulky, overgrown, uncouth figure, a primordial giant from the Stone Age. And since there have been a number of apocryphal stories regarding the source of Mr. Davenport's inspiration, it will not be without interest to print the artist's own statement. "As a matter of fact," he says, "I got the idea in St. Mark's Square in Venice. Seeing a flock of pigeons flying about in that neighborhood I immediately, with my love of birds and beasts, determined by fair means or foul to purloin a pair. I watched them fly hither and thither, and in following them came across a statue of Samson throwing some man or other—I forget his name—to the ground. The abnormal size of the muscles of the figure struck me at once, and turning round to my wife, who was with me, I said with a sudden inspired thought, 'The Trusts!'"

DAVENPORT'S CONCEPTION OF THE TRUSTS.

Of equal importance are the various series in lighter vein through which Mr. Opper aims to lead people to the same way of thinking politically as the paper which he serves. Long years of labor and constant production do not seem to have in any way drained his power of invention, for no sooner has one series done its work, and before the public has become sated with it, than an entirely new line of cartoons is introduced.   Mr. Opper, as well as Mr. Davenport, has had his fling at and drawn his figure of the Trusts, and to place the two figures side by side is to contrast the methods and work of the men.   Mr. Opper's purpose seems to be, first of all, to excite your mirth, and consequently he never fails to produce a certain effect.   When you take up one of his cartoons in which the various stout, sturdy, and well-fed gentlemen typifying the different Trusts are engaged in some pleasant game the object of which is the robbing, or abusing of the pitiable, dwarfish figure representative of the Common People, your first impulse is a desire to laugh at the ludicrous contrast.   It is only afterwards that you begin to think seriously how badly the abject little victim is being treated, and what a claim he has upon your sympathy and indignation. In those series which are designed entirely along party lines, such as " Willie and his Papa," this method is even more effective, since it begins by disarming party opposition.

Of such men, and the younger draughtsmen of to-day, much more might be written with sympathetic understanding and enthusiasm.   But most of them belong rather to the century that has just begun rather than that which has lately closed, and a hundred years from now, whoever attempts to do for the twentieth century a service analogous to that which has here been undertaken for the nineteenth, will find an infinitely ampler and richer store of material, thanks to this group of younger satirists in the full flood of their enthusiasm, who are valiantly carrying on the traditions of the men of the past—of Leech and Tenniel, of Daumier, and Philipon, and Cham and André Gill, of Nast and Keppler and Gillam, and who have already begun to record with trenchant pencil the events that are ushering in the dawn of the new century.

THE END